Creating 3D Models for 3D Printing Using OpenSCAD

by

David Leithauser

Table of Contents

Introduction

Today, 3D printers are becoming more popular and useful. I use them for everything from prototyping my inventions to making custom parts to repair household items to making custom Christmas ornaments. There are many varieties of 3D printers, but one thing they all have in common is that to print something, you need to use a 3D modeling program to create a model. This model is then saved in a special 3D format, most commonly the STL format. Once you have this file, you usually have to run it through a slicer program that converts it to gcode that your printer can understand.

There are many software programs to create the 3D models and save them as STL or other graphic files. Most modeling programs are graphically operated, where you essentially draw the object using your mouse. This has some advantages, but also some drawbacks. Sometimes it can be hard to draw the 3D object on the 2D screen, with the object being stretched or moved in a different direction than you want. It can sometimes be hard to create some shapes because you are trying to maneuver a 3D object using a 2D display. You may try to move in one direction, but the software interprets your mouse movement on the screen as going in another direction. It can also be hard getting exact dimensions, since you are trying to manually stretch or move objects on your screen with a mouse.

OpenSCAD is a totally free program that takes a different approach. Instead of drawing the object by hand, it lets you describe it by telling it to create a shape like a sphere, cylinder, box, etc., and position it at a certain location. You can then add objects, alter them by doing things like stretching them, cutting away portions, and other operations that give you considerable control of the final product, all by simply writing what you want to do with the objects. This allows for considerable precision.

You can view the object you are creating at any time to see how it is going so far.

In this book, I will take you through the process of creating 3D models with OpenSCAD in a step-by-step manner that I think you will find easy to follow. I will concentrate on the aspects that I find most useful for generating 3D models suitable for 3D printing. I will not get into aspects of OpenSCAD designed to make pictures or 3D movies, such as coloring objects or animation, unless they have some use as a modeling design tool.

I will end the book with a series of chapters called the project section that describe how to make a variety of actual objects that you can use. These give you examples of how to put together the techniques I have discussed in the earlier chapters and also provide useful components like connectors and moving parts that you can incorporate in your own projects.

I will be using OpenSCAD version 2019.05 for Windows in this book. OpenSCAD is also available for MacOS and Linux. Although I will not be discussing those in this book, most of what I have written should apply to those versions too.

Chapter 1

Getting Started with OpenSCAD

In this chapter, I will tell you how to install OpenSCAD and go over the basic operations like loading and saving files, viewing the objects you are creating, and other fundamentals. I will hold off on how to actually create objects until Chapter 2.

As I mentioned, OpenSCAD is a totally free program. The first step is to download and install it on your computer. Go to the Web site https://www.openscad.org/downloads.html You will see a box labeled Windows with four squares inside it. The two on the left download an executable file, while the two on the right download a ZIP file. I recommend downloading the executable file, since installation is much simpler. The ones on the top download the version for 32-bit computers, and the ones on the bottom download the version for 64-bit computers. If you do not know which computer you have, type system in the Windows box that says "Type here to search" and that will allow you to run the System information program that will tell you. If you still cannot determine I suggest you click on the top left box. The one for 32-bit computers will usually run fine on 64-bit computers, although the 64-bit version will run better. After you click on the appropriate box, the file will be downloaded. Run the executable file to install OpenSCAD.

Once OpenSCAD is installed, run the program. A screen will pop up asking if you want New (create a model from scratch), Open (open a saved model), or Help (open a web page with instructions. There is a box labeled Recents that will list files you recently created and saved, but this will be empty now. There is also a list of directories with sample files. For now, click on New to get an empty setup. The screen will look like this.

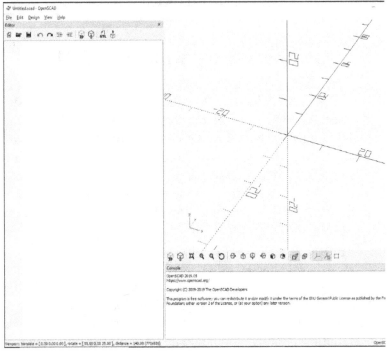

Figure 1.1

On the left side of the screen, you will see a large empty box. This is the text box where you will put the text that describes your model. I will frequently refer to this text as your model code, or simply code throughout this book, and the text area as the code area. On the right you will see a larger box with a coordinate system. In the lower left corner, there is also a small marker showing the X, Y, and Z directions. This is viewing area where you will be able to see the model that you create or load. Below this you will see some small icons that help you control the view, which I will explain shortly. Below this is a report box where OpenSCAD reports results of what it is doing, including error messages. At the top you will see a standard menu bar, with options File, Edit, Design, View, and Help.

Just to help demonstrate the viewing, let's load a sample model. Click on the Files menu and a dropdown menu will appear. Move down and click on examples, then click on basics when that appears, and then click on CSG.scad. This will load the CSG sample model (all models have the extensions scad). You should now see a lot of text in the text box. Press the F5 key, and three odd-looking objects should appear in the viewing area.

First, let's rotate and move the view of the model. Place the mouse in the center of the viewing area and then press and hold the left mouse button. Move the mouse right or left to rotate the model. Move the mouse up or down to tilt the model. To move the model instead of rotating it, press and hold the right mouse button while you move the mouse courser around the viewing area. Note that these actions do not actually change the model, only your view of it. For example, if you shifted the view so that the model appears to be on its side, that does not mean the model would print on its side once you create the STL file. This applies to all the techniques I am describing for shifting your view.

Next, look at the little icons below the viewing area. On the left, you will see an icon that looks like a box with two > signs on it. This is the preview icon. If you make any changes in the code, clicking on this icon will cause the revised model to be shown in the viewing area, However, you can get the same effect by pressing the F5 key, which I find easier than clicking on the icon. Next to this icon, there is an icon that looks like a box with an arrow putting down. This will render your model. That is, is will actually create the 3D model ready to save to an STL file, as opposed to the preview process which merely creates a picture of what it will look like. You can also render it by pressing the F6 key, which again I find easier. Once it is rendered, the rendered version of your model will appear in the viewing window. This may look a little different than the preview, and will actually be more accurate. Rendering the model does not automatically generate or save the STL file. To do that, you can press the F7 key or go to the Files menu, go down to export, and then over to "Export as STL." Either way, a typical Windows file menu will appear that lets you name the STL file and select where you want to put it.

The third icon below the viewing window looks like a magnifying glass with arrows pointing away from it. This is the "View All" icon. Clicking on this automatically zooms the viewing window so it shows your entire model. (You can also get the same effect by holding down both the Shift and Ctrl keys and pressing the V key.) If your model is so big that you cannot see the entire model, it zooms out. If the model is very small, it zooms in for a closer look. The next icon is a magnifying glass with a + sign in it. This zooms in on the model so you can see part of it up closer. The next icon is a magnifying glass with a - sign in it. This zooms out so you can see more of the model. The next icon looks like an arrow going counterclockwise. Click on this, and the model view returns to the default position, the one you first saw when you previewed it. The next six icons switch the model to various set view positions, like top, bottom, right, front, etc.

The next two set the view as perspective or orthogonal, which makes a very small difference in how objects in the distance look. I find these two trivial. The third icon from the right turns on and off the axis lines and distance numbers, and the second one from the right leaves the axis lines but removes the numbers. I find these axis lines and numbers useful and do not recommend turn them off. I believe that the four icons described in this paragraph are for people who are using OpenSCAD to create models for pictures, not for 3D printing.

The last icon shows the edges of all the little pieces your model is actually made of. This can be useful if you want a better idea of how high your resolute in on curved or rounded surfaces, something I will describe in upcoming chapters.

The effects of these icons can also be found in the dropdown menu under View on the top menu. Two other viewing options on the View menu not provided by icons are wireframe and thrown together. Wireframe shows one the edges of each component. This can be useful to look inside the model to see any pieces hidden by the walls, a sort of x-ray vision view of the model. Thrown together view shows you pieces that will not be part of the model because they are used for subtracting or removing parts of the other components. I will get into this in later chapters. For now, I encourage you to play around with these functions until you are familiar with them before you build any models.

When you have created a model, you will want to save it. To do this, click on the Files top menu and then Save, or press Ctrl-S, or just click on the picture of the floppy disk (third icon from the left just under the top menu). A file screen will appear that allows you to input a name and select a file location. In the file name text box, input a name for your project. Next, you need to select the folder location. You will have to change from the current location, because the default location is actually a protected folder that you cannot write to on most Windows computers. I strongly suggest that you first go to the documents folder. Scroll through this folder, and you will actually find a folder named OpenSCAD that was created when you installed OpenSCAD. Double-click on this to open this folder. I suggest that you then click on the "New Folder" button near the top of the window. This will create a new folder named (unimaginatively) "New Folder." Left click on this and select rename from the drop-down menu. You can then give the folder a nice name like "My stuff" or another name. You will only have to do this once. After you have created this folder, I suggest that you go there whenever you want to save a file. If you want to save a file with modifications without overwriting the original file, you can use the Save As function under the Files top menu.

Now that we have the mechanics out of the way, let's make models.

Chapter 2

Basic 3D shapes

In this chapter, I will explain most of the simple basic 3D shapes you can build with a single command. I will get to more elaborate shapes, as well as moving things around and other techniques, in later chapters.

cube

Let's start out with a simple cube. In the code area, type

```
cube(10);
```

and press ENTER. This describes a cube 10 mm on a side. All measurements are in mm in OpenSCAD. Note the semicolon on the end. All executable statements in OpenSCAD must end with a semicolon. This simply tells OpenSCAD that this is the end of the statement or command.

Note that nothing visible happens when you type this. Once you have finished typing, you still need to press F5 or click on the preview icon or click on Preview under the View menu to actually see what you have created. Go ahead and press the F5 key on your keyboard. You should now see the cube. Congratulations. You have just created your first model. Feel free to spin it around just to see it from all sides. BTW, you will see that it just comes up to the markers on the axes, since each marker is 10 mm. You might also notice that the cube extends 10 mm in the X, Y, and Z directions, with one corner at the origin.

Now if all you could do with the cube command were to make a perfectly square cube, it would not be very useful. Fortunately, you can specify the dimensions for

length, width, and height individually. Erase the cube(10); command and replace it with
cube([20, 10, 2]);

Press the F5 button again. You will see a long, narrow, flat box. The box is 20 mm in the X direction, 10 mm in the Y direction, and 2 mm high. Note that you need to enclose the three numbers in square brackets. This, to put it simply, is because the cube command is expecting only one number. By enclosing the numbers in brackets, you are turning the three numbers into one number, a vector (a three-dimensional number). If that confuses you, just skip the technical explanation and remember that when you use three numbers to specify different dimensions (which you will almost always do), you need to enclose them in square brackets.

There is one other parameter you can use with the cube command. As mentioned before, the cube normally has one corner at the origin and extends out the specified amount in the X, Y, and Z directions. You can case it to be centered on the origin by adding the center = true statement like this
cube([10, 20, 5], center = true);
Try this (don't forget to hit the F5 key) and rotate box around on the screen with the mouse. You will see that it is centered in all three directions. I do not normally recommend doing this, because if you forget to move it up above the XY plane (which will be explained later), your model will actually be below the print bed on your 3D printer. Some slicers and/or printers will automatically move it above the print bed, but a few do not and will damage the print bed or extruder trying to print below the print bed.

You can (and undoubtedly will) make models with more than one component. In simple cases, this means simply adding more items to the code. Try putting this into the code box.
cube([30, 10, 5]);
cube([20, 10, 10]);

cube([10, 10, 15]);

After you press the F5 key, you will see a stairway as shown in Figure 2.1.

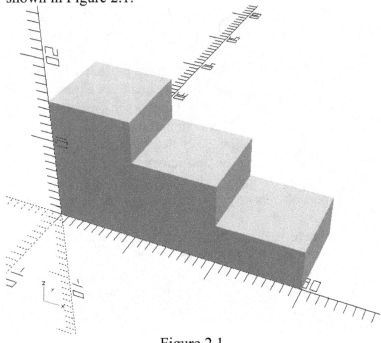

Figure 2.1

This consists of one long low cube, one medium length taller cube, and one short even taller cube, all starting at the same place. This should give you an idea of how you will be building complex models.

In this example, we used numbers for the cube parameters. You can also create and use defined constants. A defined constant is simply a name you give to a number. This is not a variable like in some programming languages. Once you define a name as meaning a number, you cannot change it. There are a few places in OpenSCAD where you can use variables, like the for operator, which I will get into later. Using defined constants can make it easy to change the shape of your model. For example, create a defined constant H in our steps.

H = 5;

```
cube([30, 10, H]);
cube([20, 10, 2 * H]);
cube([10, 10, 3 * H]);
```
This makes the first step H (5) mm tall, the second step twice as tall from the ground, etc. Thus, each step is automatically the same height above the previous step. You can now automatically change the height of every step just by changing the value of H. You could likewise define W as being 10 and replace the second parameter with W so that you can change the width of every step at once, and so on. Try putting in this code, changing the value of H several times, and pressing the F5 key after each change to observe the effect. Note that you do need the semicolon at the end of the defined constant assignment command.

One other quick note. The OpenSCAD language is case sensitive. Be sure to use all lower case for the word cube and all other keywords or your will get an error message. Defined constants can be capitalized, and I find this useful in distinguishing defined constants from keywords in my code.

sphere

The next basic shape is the sphere. The basic command for this is
```
sphere(radius);
```
where radius is any number. Clear the cube commands from the code box and put in
```
sphere(10);
```
Then press F5. You should see a sphere 10 mm in radius centered at the origin. Unlike the cube command, sphere automatically centers the sphere at the origin rather than putting it above the XY plane.

Note that I said the radius is 10 mm because you input just 10 as a parameter. If you prefer to use the diameter instead of the radius as the parameter, you can specify this by using d =, like this.
```
sphere(d = 10);
```

This simply tells OpenSCAD that you want the number to be the diameter instead of the radius.

You may notice that the sphere looks a little rough, with lot of square faces rather than a smooth sphere. This is because any 3D modeling program actually creates an object out of flat surfaces. They are incapable of actually making completely rounded surfaces. Does this mean you are stuck with the roughness you see in this sphere? No. You can increase the resolution of your sphere, telling OpenSCAD to make the sphere out of more, smaller flat surfaces. You do this by adding the $fn parameter, called the resolution parameter. Try changing the sphere command to

sphere(d = 10, $fn = 50);

After you press the F5 key, you will see the sphere become much smoother. For a sphere, the $fn value is actually the number of pieces (squares) going around the sphere once from one point around the sphere and back again. Now try other higher numbers, like 100. The higher the number, the greater the resolution, but the longer it will take to preview or render the model. OpenSCAD does not recommend values over 100 for $fn, but I find that if you only have a few spheres or other objects using $fn, you can use larger values. I often use 999 for objects that require precise tolerances, but I admit that might be a bit excessive.

Although you can use a higher value of $fn to make the sphere smoother, you can also use lower values to create shapes other than a sphere with the sphere command. For example, a value of 4 gives a cube, which is not particularly useful since you already can make a cube with the cube command. Just for fun, try some other values like 5 or 6 to see the shapes you get.

You can also use two other parameters, $fs and $fa, to change the shape of the sphere. $fa sets the minimum angle for the fragments, and $fs sets the minimum size. However, I frankly find these much less useful and much harder to work with than $fn, so I will skip the discussion

14

of those. I have found no effect I can achieve with either of those that I cannot achieve more easily with $fn.

As with the cube and all the shapes and operations, you can use a defined constant in place of a number in the sphere command. If you have multiple spheres or other objects like cylinders (see below) that use $fn, you can also simply set the value of $fn at the beginning of your code as a defined constant with a statement like $fn = 99;. Every object in your model will then use this value of $fn unless you specify a different $fn value for that object within its parenthesis.

cylinder

The cylinder command looks like this.
cylinder(h = 10, r = 5);
This would create a cylinder of height 10 mm and radius 5 mm. Create one of these to see what it looks like. Play around with the parameter values if you like to get a feel for it. Incidentally, you can also use d = instead of r = to make the number the diameter instead of the radius of the cylinder.

Like the sphere, you will notice that the cylinder is not completely smooth. Like the sphere, you can add the $fn = parameter to smooth the cylinder. The value of $fn will be the number of sides around the cylinder. Try this:
cylinder(h = 10, r = 5, $fn = 50);
You will see a much smoother cylinder, and you can use higher numbers like 100 to get a smoother cylinder. On the other hand, using lower numbers for $fn can be particularly useful for cylinders. For example, $fn = 6 gives you a hexagonal figure, and $fn=3 gives you an equilateral triangle. These are shown in Figure 2.2.

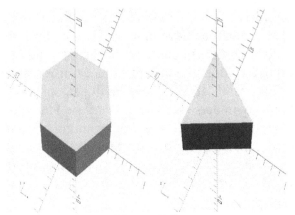

Figure 2.2

There is another parameter for cylinder that makes it very flexible for making shapes. As you recall, we specified the radius with the r = parameter. This causes the cylinder to be the same radius top to bottom. However, you can instead name the top and bottom radii separately, creating a shape that is not the same radius at the top and bottom by specifying r1 and r2, like this:

cylinder(h = 20, r1 = 10, r2 = 5);

You can even make r2 = 0, forming a cone. Figure 2.3 shows these.

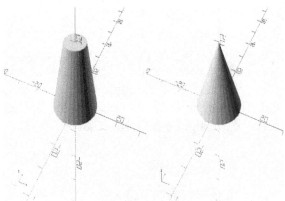

Figure 2.3

You can combine this with low $fn values to produce even more useful shapes. Since $fn = 4 would give you a cube and r2 = 0 narrows the top to a point, you get a pyramid from something like
cylinder(h = 10, r1 = 10, r2 = 0, $fn = 4);
This gives you this:

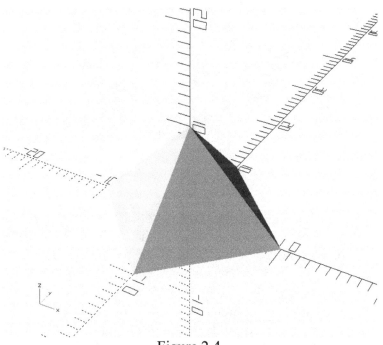

Figure 2.4

A value of $fn = 3 will give you a four-sided figure with each side being an equilateral triangle. I will leave it to you to create and view this, just for fun.

Getting back to regular cylinders with a fair number of sides for a moment, there is one point that could use clarification. Since the cylinder is not an exact circle as seen from the top, is it bigger or smaller than a circle? The answer is normally smaller. The tips of the edges touch the edge of the circle, with the rest of the cylinder inside. Figure 2.5 shows a 6-sided cylinder of radius r made by OpenSCAD superimposed on a real circle of radius r.

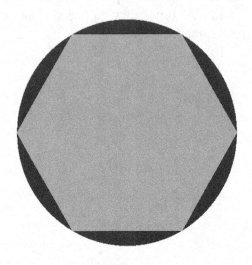

Figure 2.5

This can be important if you are making precision pieces, especially if you are using the cylinder command to cut out a hole (which will be explained later). Of course, the more sides you have (higher value of $fn), the closer the cylinder will be to the size of a circle. However, if you want to make the cylinder be outside the circle of the same radius, you can do this by multiplying the radius by 1/cos(180/fn), where fn is the value of $fn. Here is an example:

```
fn = 6;
MakeOutside = 1 / cos(180 / fn);
cylinder(h = 2, r = 2 * MakeOutside, $fn = fn);
```

This makes a 6-sided cylinder of radius 2 that is outside a circle of radius 2, as shown in Figure 2.6.

Figure 2.6

    As with the sphere, you can also use $fa and $fs parameters to control the number of sides of the cylinder. However, as before, I find these so limited and confusing to work with and $fn so much easier and more intuitive that I am not going to bother to get into a discussion of $fa or $fs here.

    There is one other parameter of cylinder you can use. Like the cube, you can add center = true to the cylinder parameters, like

cylinder(h = 5, r = 2, center = true);

However, the cylinder is automatically centered at 0 on the X and Y axes and centering it on the Z axis is seldom useful, so I never really find use for this. In addition, in later chapters I will be discussing a way to move any object any amount in any direction, so this command is redundant.

polyhedron

One very powerful and versatile object for building models with a lot of flat surfaces is the polyhedron. This basically lets you build any object with any shapes of flat surfaces. The downside, as you might expect from something so flexible, is that it can be very complex to use.

To make a polyhedron, you must first list all the corners of the polyhedron. A corner is any point in space where three or more surfaces meet. After you list all the corners, you must you trace out the path around each surface. To do this you list all the surfaces by listing all the corners of the surface in the correct order. Sounds complicated? It is.

Let's say you want to make the fairly simple shape in Figure 2.7.

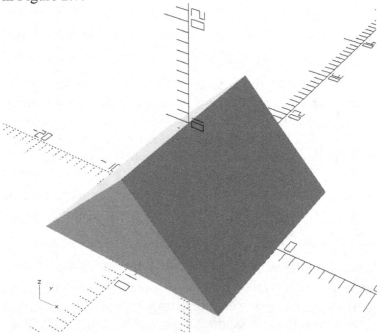

Figure 2.7

This has six corners. Coordinates are always listed in the format [X,Y,Z], so these corners are at the following coordinates: [-10,-10,0], [10,-10,0], [10,10,0], [-10,10,0],

20

[0,-10,10], and [0,10,10]. The first four are in the XY plane, and the last two are the top corners 10 mm above the XY plane. To list these in the polyhedron, you would use the following format.

```
polyhedron(
[
[-10, -10, 0],
[10, -10, 0],
[10, 10, 0],
[-10, 10, 0],
[0, -10, 10],
[0, 10, 10]
]
```

First, I should explain that in OpenSCAD, spacing and line breaks mean nothing. You can put as many spaces or line breaks in the middle of a command as you like and it will not affect the way OpenSCAD executes the command. I have divided up the command into separate lines to make it easier to keep track of each part.

You have the polyhedron keyword, followed by the parenthesis. The entire set of parameters will be enclosed in parentheses. I have not put in the closing parenthesis because the command is not finished. Next you have an opening square bracket, which is the start of enclosing all the corner points you are about to list. Next you have the first point, [10,-10,0], enclosed in square brackets. The list of points must be separated by commas, so you have a comma after this. I have then repeated this with each of the other corner points. Finally, we have the closing bracket that indicates the end of the list of points. Note that there is no comma after the last point, since you are not separating that from another point.

You will be referring to these points by number. To make it more confusing and counterintuitive, the first point is numbered 0 instead of 1, so the numbers of the points are 0 through 5. I find it well worth numbering the points to help refer to them in the next step, defining the surfaces using these points. To do this, I find it very useful to use what is called commenting the code. If you put two slash marks (/) in your code, the slash marks and everything after them are ignored by OpenSCAD. Therefore, you can write the above lines line this without affecting the execution of the code.

```
polyhedron(
[
[-10, -10, 0], // point 0
[10, -10, 0],  // point 1
[10, 10, 0],   // point 2
[-10, 10, 0], // point 3
[0, -10, 10],  // point 4
[0, 10, 10] // point 5
]
```

Now you can more easily see what the number of each point is.

The next step is the list of paths around the surfaces. You need a comma next to separate the list of points from the list of surfaces, then another opening square bracket to start enclosing the list of surfaces, so you have this.

```
polyhedron(
[
[-10, -10, 0], // point 0
[10, -10, 0],  // point 1
[10, 10, 0],   // point 2
[-10, 10, 0], // point 3
[0, -10, 10],  // point 4
[0, 10, 10] // point 5
]
,
[
```

Listing 2.1

Now for the first surface. Let's start with the bottom first. List the points starting with any one of the four bottom points going around clockwise as seen from the bottom. In this case, I happen to have listed the points in exactly the order you need them, so the first surface can be written as [0,1,2,3]. Since you can start with any point, you could just as easily have written [2,3,0,1]. In any case, this was the easy one.

Now let's do the triangle on the side facing us. Let's arbitrarily start with the corner that is at lower left side, the point at [-10,-10,0]. This is point 0 on our list. The next point clockwise is the top of the triangle at [0,-10,10]. This is point 4. The next point going around the triangle is point 1. So, the triangle facing you is [0,4,1].

Now let's do one more for demonstration, the triangle on the back face, the one that is hidden in Figure 2.7. Let's arbitrarily start with the corner that is at [10,10,0], the lower left corner as seen facing that side from the outside, which is the opposite direction from the way we are viewing in Figure 2.7. This is point 2. The next point going clockwise is the top point of the triangle, point 5 on the list. The final point is point 3, so the description of this surface is [2,5,3]. There are two more surfaces to define, but you should have the idea by now I will not take up any more space here explaining these. When you have defined all the surfaces, you need to list them just as you listed the points. Listing 2.2 shows this.

```
polyhedron(
[
[-10, -10 ,0], // point 0
[10, -10, 0], // point 1
[10, 10, 0], // point 2
[-10, 10, 0], // point 3
[0, -10, 10], // point 4
[0, 10, 10] // point 5
]
,
```

```
[
[0, 1, 2, 3],
[0, 4, 1],
[2, 5, 3],
[3, 5, 4, 0],
[1, 4, 5, 2]
]
);
```

Listing 2.2

You can see that after the opening bracket that enclosed the list of surfaces, we have each surface listed. Each surface except the last one is followed by a comma. The last one is followed by the closing square bracket that marks the end of the list of surfaces, followed by the closing parenthesis for the polyhedron command, followed by the semicolon that follows all commands.

You now have the complete polyhedron command. Remember that the comments and line breaks were just to make it easier to keep track of everything, so the command in Listing 2.1 could have been written as

polyhedron([[-10, -10, 0],[10, -10, 0],[10, 10, 0],[-10, 10, 0],[0, -10, 10],[0, 10, 10]],[[0, 1 , 2, 3],[1, 4, 0],[2, 5, 3],[3, 5, 4, 0],[1, 4, 5, 2]]);

This was a fairly simple polyhedron, consisting of only six corner points and five surfaces. There is basically no limit that I know of to how complex you can build these, as long as you can visualize it.

The two things that are most likely to trip you up are remembering that the first point is numbered 0 (since you would intuitively expect it to be 1) and getting the order of the points of a surface in the right order, including clockwise. If you put them in a totally wrong order, you will get a totally weird shape, usually with a hole in it. Figure 2.8 shows what you would get if you wrote the last surface as [1, 5, 4, 2] instead of [1, 4, 5, 2].

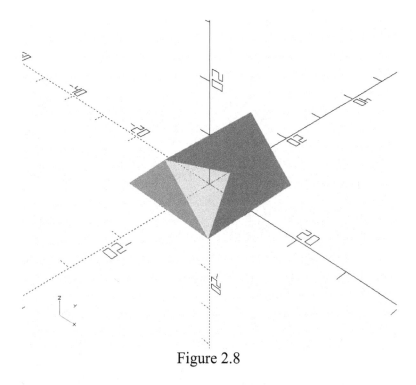

Figure 2.8

Regarding the less obvious mistake of listing the point counterclockwise instead of clockwise, there is a trick to find any surface where you made this mistake. Instead of pressing F5 to view the model, press F12 to get the thrown together view. This will show any surface you defined counterclockwise in a purple or pink color instead of yellow.

I have one other suggestion when constructing polyhedrons. After you have written the code for the corner points as shown in Listing 2.1, add all the bracket, parenthesis, and semicolon in the last two lines of Listing 2.2, leaving a few blank lines before those last two lines. Then add the surfaces one by one (remember no comma after the last one) and press F5 or F12 key as you add each surface. This will allow you to see each surface as you

25

construct it, so you can see immediately if there is any problem. This is easier than looking at a completed by incorrect polyhedron and trying to figure out which line of code is wrong.

union

You have seen that you can simply list multiple components of a model to add together parts, as we did in the staircase in Figure 2.1. You can actually join multiple shapes into one compound shape with the union command. Using this on the code that generated Figure 2.1, it would look like this.

```
union(){
    cube([30, 10, 5]);
    cube([20, 10, 10]);
    cube([10, 10, 15]);
}
```

Simply put union(){ before the group of objects and } after them. This joins the objects into one. If this were all you do, there would be no change in the resulting model. However, there will be times when you want to move, rotate, or otherwise perform an operation on multiple elements all at once in unison, and joining multiple elements into element one allows you to do this. I will give examples of doing this in later chapters, but I wanted to lay the foundation here before we get to those.

Chapter 3

3D text

In this chapter, I will discuss another element you can create, 3D text. This enables you to create objects like the nametags shown in figure 3.1.

Figure 3.1

The tag on the top has text extruding from the surface, while the tag on the bottom has the text cut into the surface. Of course, two-color objects require a two-color printer. I used a Geeetech A10M to produce these, which allows you to change colors in the gcode partway through the print. I will not get into that in this book, since that is another subject altogether.

The basic command for creating text is just
text("Your text here");

If you input this into your code window and press F5 and then the View All icon, you will see this.

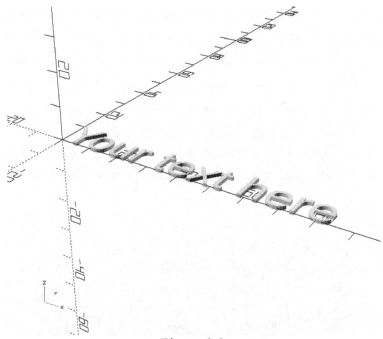

Figure 3.2

If you rotate this around and look at it, this gives the impression that the text is 1 mm high and centered on the Z-axis. This is not true. The text is actually flat two-dimensional. To get a true picture of what the text is like, press the F6 key to actually render it and you will see true text as shown in Figure 3.3.

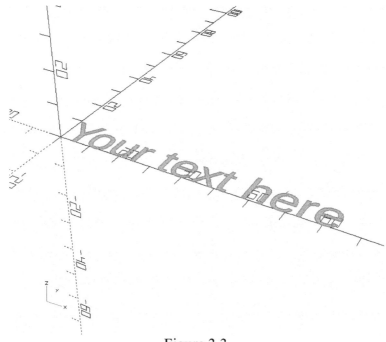

Figure 3.3

Now a two-dimensional object is of no use in 3D printing, so you need to convert it to a 3D model. You do this with the linear_extrude command. This goes before the text command. Like this
linear_extrude(height = 2) text("Your text here");
This converts the text to 3D by extruding the text upward by 2 mm. Of course, you can make it any height you want. The result of the above command is shown in Figure 3.4.

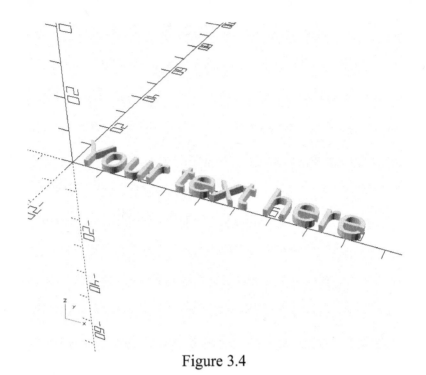

Figure 3.4

The extrude command is a very powerful tool for making 3D shapes out of 2D shapes, and I will dedicate a chapter to extrude later. For now, I have only provided the basic version that relates to text.

You can also include special characters using ASCII or Unicode characters by inserting "\x" or "\u" followed by a number in hexadecimal. I do not find the ASCII function useful at all, since you are limited to 0 through 7f, all of which are accessible from the keyboard anyway. However, the Unicode does allow you to display some hard-to-produce characters, characters like the degree symbol or the Euro or British pound symbol or Greek letters. For example,
text("Greek is \u03B1 \u03B2 \u03B3");
displays "Greek is" followed by the first three letters of the Greek alphabet. This can be useful for including all sorts of special symbols. You can look up tables of Unicode characters on the Internet, but remember that they must be

expressed as hexadecimal. One site I recommend (as of the writing of this book) is https://www.rapidtables.com/code/text/unicode-characters.html

The text command has quite a few parameters your can use besides the text itself. You can change the font, style, size spacing, etc., much like you can change these in a word processor. Here are your options, listed in what I consider decreasing order of usefulness. Of course, you would have the linear_extrude command in front of any of the examples I will list here.

$fn

I mentioned that you can include the $fn parameter in the linear_extrude command. You could instead include it in the text command to make your text smoother. Example:
text("abcdef", $fn = 99);

font and style

To change the font, use the parameter
font = "Font name:style=style type" such as
font = "Liberation Sans:style=Bold Italic"
For example:
text("Your text here", font="Arial:style=Bold");
You can find a list of all the available fonts and the styles available for each font by clicking on the Help menu at the top of the OpenSCAD screen and then on font list.

size

The format for this is size=#, where # is any number and can be a decimal number like 5.2. Example:
text("Your text here", size = 3.4);
This controls the size of the text, both the height and the width. Note that this does not affect the extrusion, only the size in the XY plane. The default value if you do not

specify the size is 10, so any number less than 10 will make the text smaller and any number larger than 10 will make the text larger.

spacing

This affects the space between text characters without affecting the actual size of the characters. Default is 1. Example:
text("Your text here", spacing = 1.5);

direction

You can control the direction your text is printed in with the direction parameter. Example:
text("Your text here", direction = "ttb");
The four options are "ltr" (left to right, the normal direction of text), "rtl" (right to left, reverse writing), "ttb" (top to bottom, going down), and "btt" (bottom to top). The default is left to right. Other than the default, the only one I see having any use is top to bottom. The right to left seems particularly worthless, especially since it does not reverse the letters, so looking at it from the other side is not readable.

halign and valign

These just move the text around. Since you can do the same thing with greater control using the translate command that I will describe in the next chapter, I will not bother to describe this at all.

language and script

These reportedly allow you to change the language and script style your text is in, but support for this is so poor I cannot even find a list of available choices.

Chapter 4

Moving Things Around

Now that we can make various types of objects, we can discuss moving them around and positioning them.

translate

The first command you can use is the translate command. The format for this is
translate([X, Y, Z])
where X, Y, and Z are number or defined constants telling you how far to move the object in the X, Y, and Z direction. The values of X, Y, and Z can be positive or negative. The translate command goes before the object you want to move and does not have a semicolon after it because it is not the end of the command. For example, suppose you want to move a 5 by 5 by 5 cube so that it is centered in the around the Z axis and sitting on the XY plane. Normally, the cube(5); command would put the cube with one corner at the origin (X = 0, Y = 0, Z = 0) extending 5 mm in the X, Y and Z directions. To put it where you want it, you would type
translate([-2.5, -2.5, 0]) cube(5);
This would pull it –2.5 mm in the X and Y directions.

Let's make a rocket sitting on a square platform. This will consist of a 40mm by 40mm by 5mm platform, a cylinder 40 mm high and 5 mm in radius, and a cone 5 mm high and 5 mm at the base. The individual command for this would be

cube([40, 40, 5]);
cylinder(h = 40, r = 5);
cylinder(h = 5, r1 = 5, r2 = 0);

However, this does not put them in the right places. Let's center the cube, move the cylinder on top it, and the cone (second cylinder) on top of that.

translate([-20, -20, 0]) cube([40, 40, 5]);
translate([0, 0, 5]) cylinder(h = 40, r = 5);
translate([0, 0, 45]) cylinder(h = 5, r1 = 5, r2 = 0);

The first translate moves the cube so it is centered by moving it half the length and width in the negative direction. The second translate moves the cylinder up 5 mm so that it sits on top the cube platform. The third translate moves the cone to the top if the cylinder. This gives you the image in Figure 4.1.

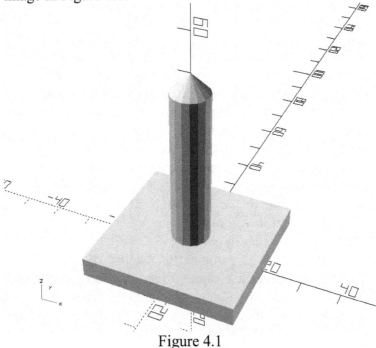

Figure 4.1

We could also have left the cube where it was and moved the cylinder and cone to it like this.

cube([40, 40, 5]);

translate([20, 20, 5]) cylinder(h = 40, r = 5);
translate([20, 20, 45]) cylinder(h = 5,r1 = 5, r2 = 0);

This gives you the same image, just in a different location. I bring this up only to clarify that there is no one set way to arrange things.

rotate

You can rotate an object around the X, Y, and/or Z axis using the rotate command in the form rotate([X,Y,Z]), where X, Y, and Z are either numbers or defined constants and are expressed in degrees, positive or negative. The first number rotates the object around the X axis, the second rotates it around the Y axis, and the third number rotates it around the Z axis.

The rotate command goes before the object to be rotated. For example:

rotate([0, -45, 0]) cube(5);

This example would have the effect of turning this

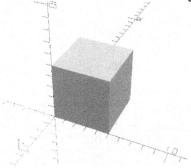

into this

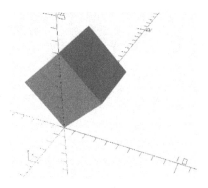

A positive number rotates the object in the clockwise direction as seen from the direction of the negative side of the axis it is being rotated around, such as a cube at the origin as seen from X = -10. Therefore, the rotate command rotate([0, -45, 0]) rotated the cube counterclockwise around the Y axis by 45 degrees. Notice that the cube was not rotated around its own center as you might intuitively expect, but around the edge on the Y-axis. Thus, the location of the object being rotated before the rotation does affect the final position of the object. For this reason, you might find it easier to predict the outcome of a rotate command if you use the center = true parameter on the object when you create it, such as cube(5, center=true); before rotating the object. This will cause the object to rotate more predictably around its own center.

The rotate command is more complicated to use than the translate command in other ways too. In the translate command, it would not matter in which order the object is moved. That is, it would not matter if it were moved in the X direction first or the Y direction first. It would end up in the same place. With the rotate command, it does matter. If you provide numbers other than 0 for all three parameters, it will first rotate the object around the X axis. It would then rotate that object, already rotated around the X axis, around the Y axis. It would then rotate the object, already rotated around the X and Y axis, around the Z axis. The resulting position would be very different than if it had rotated the object in a different order. You can change the rotation order by using the rotate command three times, each time only rotating along one axis. For example,

rotate([45, 0, 0])rotate([0, 0, 90]) rotate([0, 45, 0]) cylinder(h = 20, r = 5);

will first rotate the object 45 degrees around the Y axis, then 90 degrees around the Z axis, then 45 degrees around the X axis. You can see that the operations are being performs in reverse order of the way they are listed. This is because the operations are being performed starting with the one closest to the object, then in order succeedingly farther away from the object.

You can, of course, combine the rotate and translate commands. For example,

translate([0, 20, 10]) rotate([90, 0, 0]) cylinder(h = 2, r = 10);

This gives you the object in Figure 4.2.

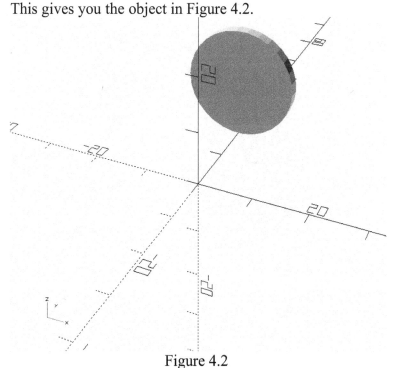

Figure 4.2

You have created a disk using the cylinder command, flipped it up on its edge by rotating it 90 degrees around the X axis, then moved it up 10 mm and 20 mm on the Y axis, making a wheel. Now let's add a few things.

translate([0, 20, 10])rotate([90, 0, 0])cylinder(h = 2, r = 10);
translate([0, -20, 10]) rotate([90, 0, 0]) cylinder(h = 2, r = 10);
translate([0, -20, 10]) rotate([-90, 0, 0]) cylinder(h = 40, r = 1);

You now have three cylinder objects, each rotated and moved, to give you Figure 4.3.

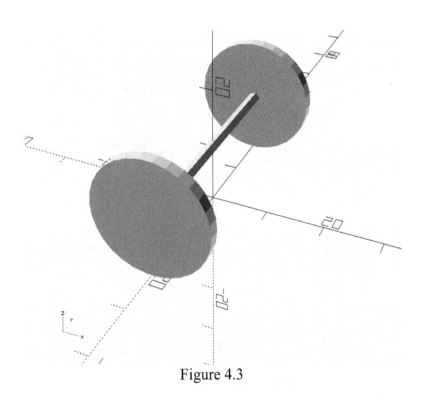

Figure 4.3

Basically, you have created a barbell, or maybe two wheels on an axle. This may seem trivial, but it demonstrates how you can combine several elements into a complete object by creating each one, then rotating and/or translating them to put them all into position. You are now well on your way to building complete models.

Chapter 5

Subtracting Parts of Objects

In previous chapters, we have seen how to build objects by combining various 3D shapes. It is also possible to cut away parts of existing shapes to form new shapes. There are two basic methods: difference and intersection.

difference

The difference command is written like this:
difference(){
    object 1;
    object 2;
    object 3;
etc.
}

Every place that any of the objects after object 1 occupy the same space as object 1, they cancel out and leave nothing. For example, if you put a cylinder inside a larger cube object, the cube object will have a hole in it where the cylinder is. Consider the following code:

cube([10, 30, 20]);
translate([10, 0, 0]) sphere(10);
translate([-10, 15, 10]) rotate([0, 90, 0]) cylinder(h = 50, r = 5);

Figure 5.1 shows what these three objects look like.

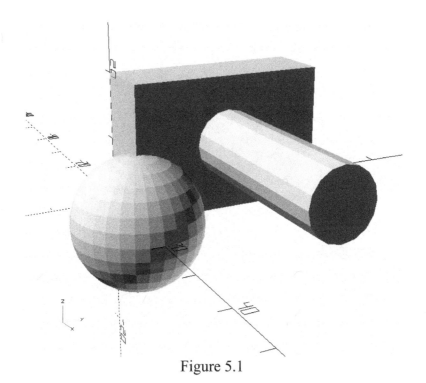

Figure 5.1

However, if you add the difference command like this

```
difference(){
   cube([10, 30, 20]);
   translate([10, 0, 0]) sphere(10);
   translate([-10,15,10]) rotate([0,90,0])
   cylinder(h = 50, r = 5);
}
```

then it looks like this

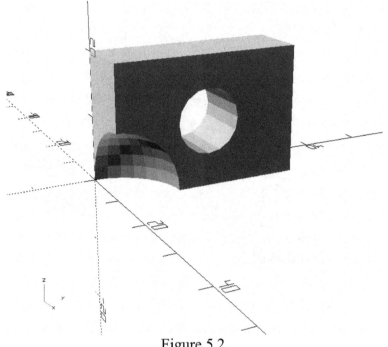

Figure 5.2

Instead of adding the sphere and cylinder, the sphere now cuts out a section of the corner and the cylinder pokes a hole through the cube. You can add as many objects as you like to cut away sections. Note the closing curly braces } at the end. This marks the end of the difference command. Anything added after the } goes back to being added to the model. Anything in the code before the word difference is also added to the model and is not affected by the code within the difference command opening and closing curly braces.

Suppose you want to cut away parts of several objects together. That is, suppose you want more than one individual element like a cube to be the object that parts are cut away from. Remember that every object after the first one in the difference command is subtracted. That is one of the times when the union command comes in handy. By joining elements together with the union command, they become one object. Suppose you create the following union.

```
union(){
    cube([10, 30, 30]);
    translate([10, 7.5, 0])cube([10, 22.5, 20]);
}
```

This looks like this.

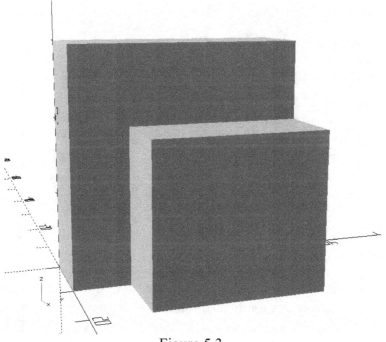

Figure 5.3

Now apply the same difference command as before to this with this code

```
difference(){
    union(){
        cube([10, 30, 30]);
        translate([10, 7.5, 0]) cube([10, 22.5, 20]);
```

```
} // End union
translate([10, 0, 0]) sphere(10);
 translate([ -10, 15, 10]) rotate([0, 90, 0]) cylinder(h =
    50, r = 5);
} // End difference
```

You now get the object in Figure 5.4.

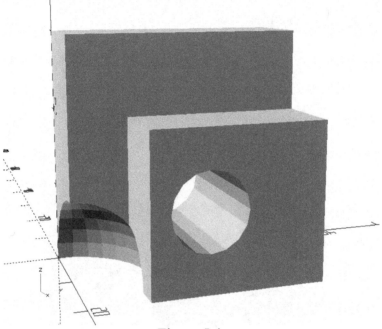

Figure 5.4

You can see that the sphere and cylinder have been cut away from both cubes, because as far as OpenSCAD is concerned, the two cubes are now one object. You can, of course, include as many individual elements in the union command as you like. You can also include as many elements after the union's closing curly braces inside the difference command to be cut away as you like.

There is an important point about the objects that you use to cut away sections from the main object. The objects you are cutting away should extend BEYOND the main object, not end at its edge. For example, to cut a hole in a cube, you might be tempted to use

```
difference(){
    cube(10);
    translate([5, 5, 0]) cylinder(h = 10, r = 2);
}
```

This code would get you this

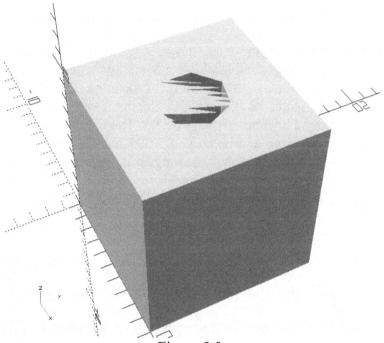

Figure 5.5

Notice the weird, jagged area where the hole is. Rotating the image would cause this area to change in appearance. The reason is that it is not clearly defined whether there is anything at the edge of the cube. Since the cylinder ends at exactly the same point as the cube starts, should that be cut away? It is not clear to OpenSCAD. The same holds true for the bottom of the cube. There may or

45

may not be an infinitely thin sheet of material where the cylinder ends. This clearly causes problems when viewing the object and can even cause a problem when the file is actually rendered for an STL file. Because of this, you should be sure the cutting away objects extend at least a little beyond the main object. The code above can be altered to read

```
difference(){
    cube(10);
    translate([5, 5, -1])cylinder(h = 12, r = 2);
}
```

Although the cube stays the same, the cylinder is now 2 mm longer and has been moved down 1 mm with the translate command (the −1 in the Z position). Note that it does not matter how much the objects used to cut away areas extend beyond the main object. The cylinder could be 10,000 mm high and be moved 5,000 mm. If you want to cut all the way through something, it is often best to make the object used to subtract much larger than necessary to make sure it goes beyond the main object.

intersection

The intersection command is somewhat the reverse of the difference command. While difference makes the model out of anything that is NOT in common with several objects, intersection accepts only what they all share. The intersection command takes any number of objects listed between opening and closing curly braces and accepts any point that falls within all the objects. Consider two objects, sphere(5) and cube(5). If you put just these in your code, you would get what you see in Figure 5.6.

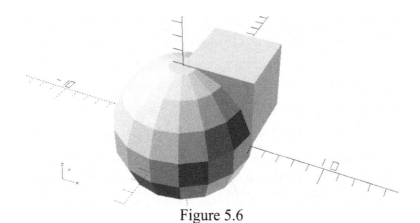

Figure 5.6

Surround these two with the intersection command, and you have the code

```
intersection(){
    sphere(5);
    cube(5);
}
```

This creates the structure in Figure 5.7.

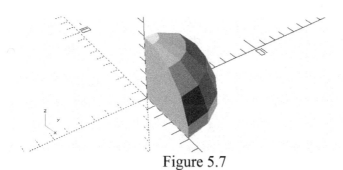

Figure 5.7

You can see that the only parts of the objects that remain are the point they had in common. If you had made the cube larger and shifted it so that it covered the entire top of the sphere, such as translate([-10,-10,0])cube(20);

you would have gotten the entire top of the sphere, a dome. Note you could have gotten the same effect with the code

```
difference(){
    sphere(5);
    translate([-10, -10, -20]) cube(20);
}
```

In that case, you would be subtracting the cube from the lower half of the sphere instead of keeping the upper part. Although you can sometimes get the same effect using difference, intersection is often easier. For example, to achieve the model in Figure 5.7, you would have needed something like

```
difference(){
    sphere(5);
    translate([-10, -10, -20]) cube(20);
    translate([-10, -20, -1]) cube(20);
    translate([-20, -10, -1]) cube(20);
}
```

By combining the various shapes and cutting pieces out of the combined shapes, you can form a wide variety of objects. In the next chapter, I will discuss distorting some of the original shapes.

Chapter 6

Distorting Objects

Once you have object, such as a sphere, you can somewhat shape them using the scale and resize commands. You can resize them completely in all dimensions, or you can distort them by selectively compressing or elongating them in only some dimensions.

scale

The scale command allows you to stretch or reduce the object relative to its original size in any or all of the three directions. The distortion is listed for the X, Y, and Z directions in that order. For example, scale([2,1,.5]) doubles the size of the object in the X direction and cuts the size in half in the Z direction by multiplying that direction by .5. Since it multiplies the Y direction by 1, the object does not change size in the Y direction. You could apply it to a sphere like this.

scale([2, 1, .5]) sphere(10);

and it would look like this

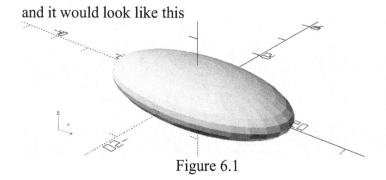

Figure 6.1

Since you can already define the size in all dimensions for cubes and polyhedrons, the only basic shapes that scale is useful for distorting are sphere and cylinder (if you want a cylinder flattened in the X or Y direction). You could also use it to distort text if you like.

In addition to using scale to distort objects, you can also use it simply to change the size of objects within a model or even the entire model itself. For example, if you have built a complex model and you decide you would like to make the entire model larger or smaller, you can surround the entire model with a scale command like this.

```
scale([2, 2, 2]){
    object code here
}
```

This will double the size of your entire model.

resize

A similar command to scale is resize. The difference is that while scale changes the size relative to the object's original size, resize sets the object to a specific size regardless of what its original size was. Suppose, for example, you created a cube that was 10 mm in the X direction and 30 mm in the Y direction and 5 mm high using cube([10, 30, 5]). Suppose you then used the resize command on to like this.

```
resize([5, 2, 10]) cube([10, 30, 5]);
```

The resulting cube would be 5 mm in the X direction and 2 mm in the Y direction and 10 mm high, regardless of the original dimensions. The resize command is useful if you want the entire object to be a very specific size once finished.

The above example distorts the object in all three dimensions. It does not retain the original ratio of X to Y to

Z. Sometimes you only want to alter one or two dimensions while leaving the remaining dimensions the same. On the other hand, you might want to set one dimension to a specific size but have the object retain the original ratio of sizes in the various dimensions so it is not distorted. You can easily do these with resize.

If you want any dimension to remain the same, put a 0 in the position for that dimension. For example, suppose you want the height to be 10 mm, but you do to want the other dimensions to change at all. You could say

```
resize([0, 0, 10]) {
    code here
}
```

If your object were cube(5), the cube would still be 5 mm in the X and Y directions, but it would then be 10 mm high.

If you want the ratio of all dimensions to be the same after setting one dimension to a specific value, put 0 in the place for the other dimensions and add auto = true, like this.

```
resize([2, 0, 0], auto = true) {
    code here
}
```

For example,

```
resize([2, 0, 0], auto = true) {
    cube(5);
}
```

would double all dimensions, resulting in a 10 mm by 10 mm by 10 mm cube. I often find it useful to make a smaller version of a model to get a faster print just to look at the product, then make a larger model of a precise size once I decide I like the look of the print. Using resize with auto = true is a great way to do that.

Chapter 7

Making 3D objects from 2D shapes

In Chapter 3, I mentioned taking a two-dimensional text image and expanding it into three dimensions using linear_extrude. In that chapter, I only discussed a straight extrusion to give the 2D text actual body. However, the linear_extrude can allow you to create some very interesting models if you employ more of the parameters. In addition, there is another extrude command, rotate_extrude, that can create even more 3D shapes from 2D patterns.

2D images

First, you need to have some knowledge of what 2D images are available to extrude. There are basically three: circle, square, and polygon. These 2d shapes are similar to their 3D equivalents.

The command for making a circle is circle(n); where n is a number or defined constant and is the radius of the circle. You can say circle(d = n); to make the number the diameter instead of the radius. The circle is centered around the Z axis and has zero depth in the Z direction.

The command for square can be either square(n); if you want a square where all sides have equal length or square([X, Y]); if you want to make a rectangle of size X in the X direction and Y in the Y direction. The square will have one corner at the X = 0 and Y = 0 position and extend in the positive direction if X and Y are positive numbers or defined constants. You can center it at the origin if you use square([X, Y], center = true);.

The polygon is usually simpler than the 3D polygon. If all you want is a solid shape, you do not need to define all the paths the way you do with a 3D polygon. You just define the points in 2 dimensions and OpenSCAD connects them in the order you list them and connects the last point to the first. For example,

polygon([[0, 0], [0, 10], [10, 10], [10, 0]]);

would create a square 10 mm on a side. Basically, you do not have to include the default path, which is to connect all the points given in the order in which they were given.

However, if you do want something more complicated than a solid figure with one path consisting of all the points connected around the outer edge, you need to define paths. For example, if you want a hole in the middle, you need to list all points, then define the path around the outside of the shape, then define the path of the points that define the hole. First you list all points, each of which consists of two numbers surrounded by square brackets, such as [0,0], separated by commas, and surround this list with square brackets like this:

[[0, 0], [20, 0], [10, 20], [5, 5], [15, 5], [10, 15]]

Then you have a comma, then you list all paths. The paths are listed the same way as the points, with each path consisting of point numbers, start with 0. The code in Listing 7.1 gives us the figure in Figure 7.1. To make it easier to read, I have broken Listing 7.1 up into separate lines, but this has no effect on how OpenSCAD interprets the code.

```
polygon(
[
[0,0], [20,0], [10,20], [5,5], [15,5], [10,15] //list of points
],
[
[0, 1, 2], [3, 4, 5] // list of paths
]
);
```
                    Listing 7.1

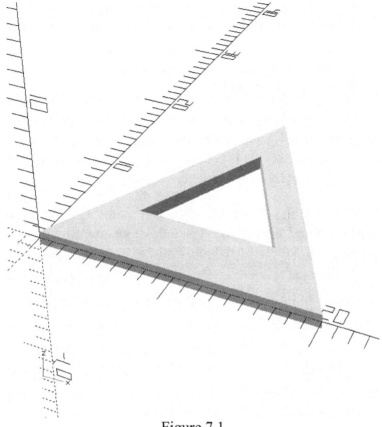

Figure 7.1

These instructions can get very confusing with all these brackets inside brackets. One trick to simplify it is to define the points and paths as simple defined constants and then list them in the polygon statement as shown in Listing 7.2.

```
P0 = [0, 0];
P1 = [20, 0];
P2 = [10, 20];
P3 = [5, 5];
P4 = [15, 5];
P5 = [10, 15];
Path1 = [0, 1, 2];
Path2 = [3, 4, 5];
```

```
polygon([P0, P1, P2, P3, P4, P5], [Path1, Path2]);
```
Listing 7.2

Here you can see that we defined each point as a defined constant called P1, P2, etc. and likewise defined the paths. (Note that you still have to refer to the points in the paths by the number of the point, starting with 0, rather than P0, P1, etc.) This is the exact same code as Listing 7.1 as far as OpenSCAD is concerned, but it makes it easier for you to keep track of the brackets, if nothing else.

You can define more holes by adding more points and connecting them as additional paths, as shown in Listing 3 and Figure 7.2. This adds four more points in a rectangular pattern linked into Path3.

```
P0 = [0, 0];
P1 = [20, 0];
P2 = [10, 20];
P3 = [5, 5];
P4 = [15, 5];
P5 = [10, 15];
P6 = [5, 2];
P7 = [15, 2];
P8 = [15, 4];
P9 = [5, 4];
Path1 = [0, 1, 2];
Path2 = [3, 4, 5];
Path3 = [6, 7, 8, 9];
polygon([P0, P1, P2, P3, P4, P5, P6, P7, P8, P9], [Path1,
Path2, Path3]);
```

Listing 7.3

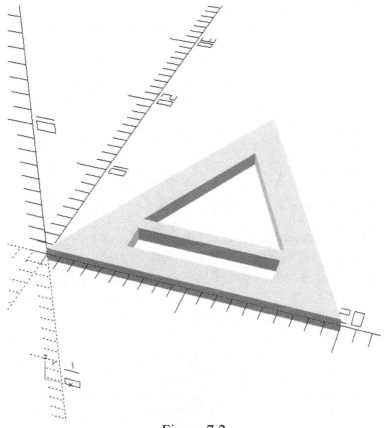

Figure 7.2

linear_extrude

The linear_extrude command can operate on any of the above 2D figures. I have already demonstrated the simple linear extrude, which extends the 2D shape upward by a set amount, such as
linear_extrude(height = 10) square(5);
which basically is simply the equivalent of
cube([5, 5, 10]);
Unless you make a really complicated 2D polygon and extend it upward or make letters as explained in Chapter 3, almost all use of a simple linear_extrude gives you a shape you could more easily have created with basic 3D shapes.

However, here are additional parameters that you can add to the linear_extrude command that do give you useful results. One example is the twist parameter, which causes the 3D object listed immediately after the linear_extrude command to twist around the Z-axis as it extrudes upward. The simple twist command is linear_extrude(height, twist = degrees) where height is the height you are extruding it and degrees is the number of degrees to rotate the shape from the bottom to the top. A positive twist twists it in the clockwise direction as seen from above. For example, rotating a centered square using this command

linear_extrude(20, twist = 180)square(5, center = true);

extrudes the square 20 mm and rotates it 180 degrees. That gives you the shape in Figure 7.3.

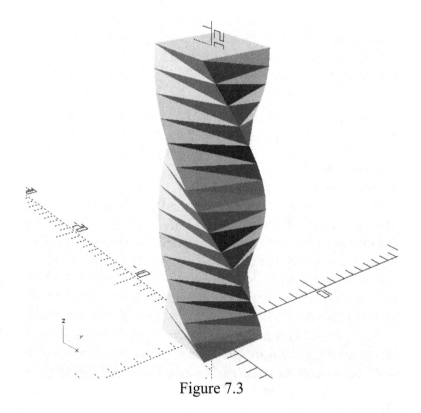

Figure 7.3

Note that this looks very blocky. The turns are actually in discrete steps, rather than smooth. You can make it smoother by adding one of several parameters. You can add the $fn parameters, or slices. These seem to have exactly the same effect, that of setting how many steps the rotation takes to make the full rotation. For example, linear_extrude(20, twist = 180, $fn = 200)
and linear_extrude(20, twist = 180, slices = 200) both have the effect of causing the rotation to occur in 200 steps, giving a much smoother figure as shown in Figure 7.4.

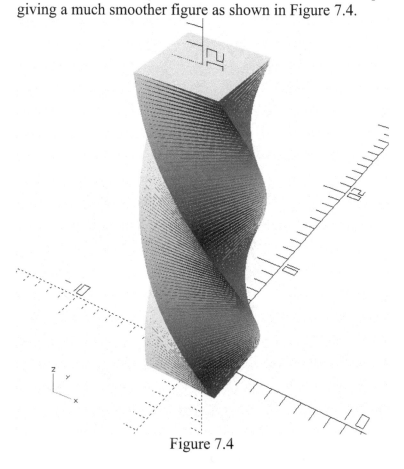

Figure 7.4

I mentioned that the rotation occurs around the Z axis. The means that not only the figure itself, but also its position gets rotated around the axis if the figure is not

centered. Let's remove the centered = true from the square command and translate it 5 mm in the X direction like this.
linear_extrude(20, twist =3 60, $fn = 200) translate([5, 0, 0]) square(5);

Now the square is far from the origin. I have also increased the rotation to 360 for more visible effect. This results in the figure in Figure 7.5.

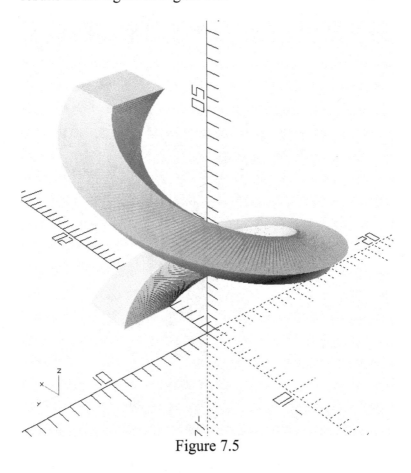

Figure 7.5

scale

Another parameter is the scale parameter, which increases or decreases the size of the shape as it extrudes upward. The value you set scale to gives the ratio of the top of the figure to the bottom. For example,

60

linear_extrude(10, scale = 0.2) square(10, center = true);
gives you a model that is 10 mm square on the bottom but
10 * .2 = 2 mm square on the top, as shown in Figure 7.6.

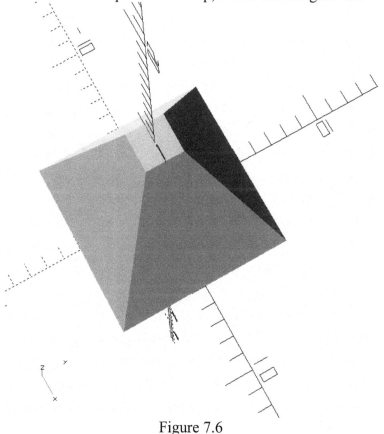

Figure 7.6

The scale function does not necessarily scale points
up from the center of the 2D shape. It works by sifting each
point of the shape relative to the Z-axis as it is extruded.
This means that if the shape is not centered, points at the
top will be less far from the Z axis than those at the bottom
if the scale value is less than 1 and farther away from the Z
axis if the scale value is greater than 1. Figure 7.7 shows
the results of this code, where the square has been moved
away from the Z axis.
linear_extrude(10, scale = 0.2) translate([10, 10])
square(10);

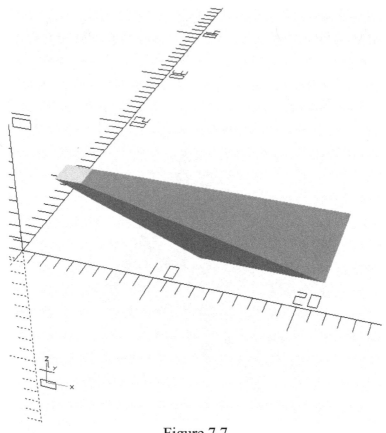

Figure 7.7

Not only is the top of the figure .2 times as big, but each point is .2 times as far from the Z axis. This may be useful in rare cases if you want the structure to slope, but is normally a problem. Therefore, it is best to make sure your shape is centered.

In the examples given so far, the scale value was just a single number, scaling equally in the X and Y directions. However, you can scale differently in the X and Y directions, like this.

linear_extrude(10, scale = [1,0]) square(10, center = true);

Here I have scaled the top all the way to 0 in the Y direction, but left the X direction at 1, making no change in the width. The result is shown in Figure 7.8. You might recognize this as the same shape we got in Figure 2.7 using a very complex polygon method, demonstrating again that there are often many ways to get a shape using OpenSCAD.

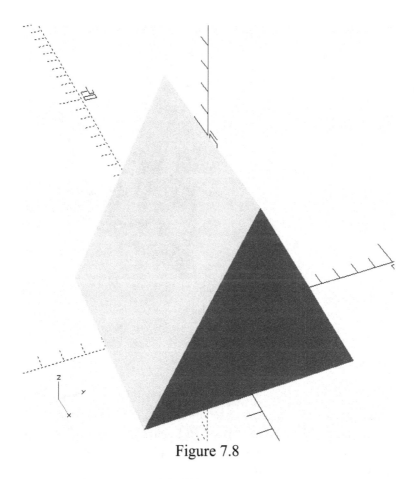

Figure 7.8

When you scale differently in the two dimensions, you can get distortion. For example, the code

```
linear_extrude(height = 10, scale = [1,0.1])
circle(10, $fn = 5);
```

gives you the shape in Figure 7.9.

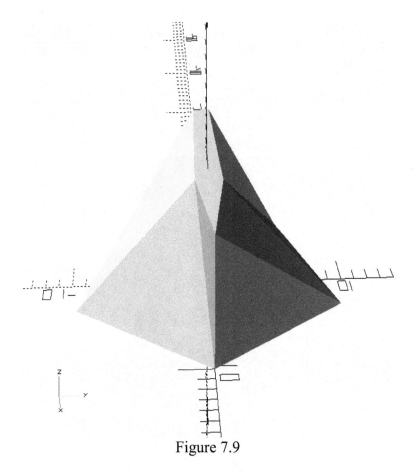

Figure 7.9

Notice that the left and right side do not match as seen from this angle. This can be fixed by increasing the slices and adding twist = 0, as in this code.

linear_extrude(height = 10, scale = [1, 0.1], slices = 90, twist=0) circle(10, $fn = 5);

which gives the corrected shape in Figure 7.10. Therefore, adding these extra slices and specifically stating twist = 0 is generally a good idea when scaling an extrusion unevenly.

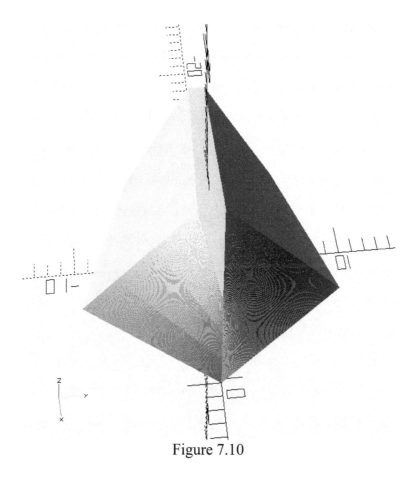

Figure 7.10

You can, of course, use scaling and twisting at the same time, creating some interesting shapes. Figure 7.11 shows the results of

linear_extrude(height = 10, scale = 0.1, twist = 90, slices = 90)
circle(5, $fn = 5);

65

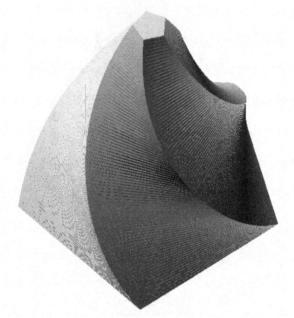

Figure 7.11

rotate_extrude

The rotate_extrude command can create even more odd shapes out of the same 2D images as the linear_extrude command. Where the linear_extrude command extends the image upward, the rotate_extrude command rotates the 2D figure 90 degrees around the X-axis and then rotates it around the Z-axis by the angle you provide. For example, Suppose you create a circle centered 2 mm from the origin using the code

translate([2, 0]) circle(r = 1, $fn = 99);

This is shown in Figure 7.12.

66

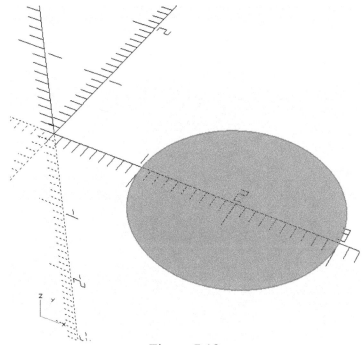

Figure 7.12

You can then flip it 90 degrees around the X axis and rotate the flipped circle around the Z axis by 360 degrees to get a torus. The code would be

```
rotate_extrude(angle = 360)
translate([2, 0])
circle(r = 1, $fn = 99);
```

and the result is shown in Figure 7.13.

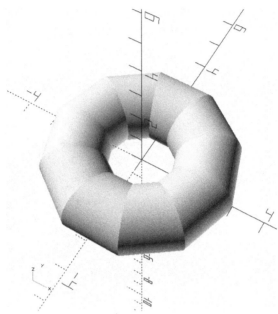

Figure 7.13

Note the angle parameter. You can make that any angle you want up to 360. For example, making it 90 gives you a quarter torus, and shown in Figure 7.14.

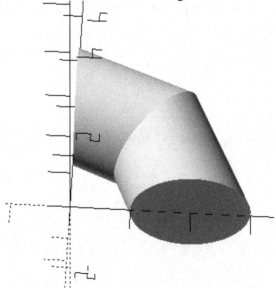

Figure 7.14

You probably notice that the torus is a bit blocky, being made up of ten segments in Figure 7.13. You may notice that I smoothed out the circle by using $fn = 99 in the circle command, but this does not affect the extrude command. If you want a nice smooth shape, you need to include a higher number for $fn in the extrude command itself, like this

rotate_extrude(angle = 360, $fn = 99) translate([2, 0]) circle(r = 1, $fn = 99);

This gives you a nice clean torus as shown in Figure 7.15. Thus, it is always good to set a fairly high $fn value within the rotate_extrude command unless you deliberately want a blocky figure.

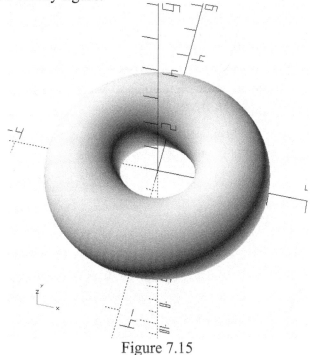

Figure 7.15

This is a simple example. You can get very interesting shapes if you use a complicated 2D structure like a polygon. However, it is important to understand the rules and the way that the extrusion will operate.

One very important rule is that the entire 2D image must be on one side of the same side of the Y-axis. That is, all points within the 2D image must be either positive or negative. If you try to rotate_extrude a figure that spans both sides of the Y-axis, like a circle that has not been translated anywhere, you will get an error message and the model will not render at all.

If the shape is just touching the Y-axis you will get a 3D shape with no hole in the middle. If there is any distance between the 2D shape and the X-axis, there will be a hole in the middle of the shape, as we saw in the torus. If the object is touching the Y-axis, the 3D shape will be on the X-Y plane. If not, the 3D shape will be suspended in the air above the X-Y plane. This would be bad for printing, unless you put some other shape under it, since 3D printers are not good at printing objects in mid-air. (Of course, many slicers will automatically put the shape on the platform, or at least give you an option to do it.)

Bearing these in mind, lets look at a few sample shapes. Take the polygon in figure 7.16.

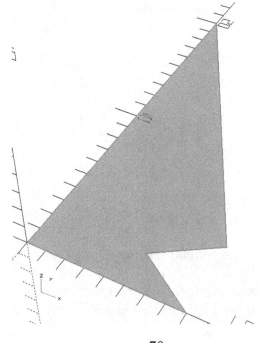

Figure 7.16

When you rotate this with rotate_extrude(angle =
360, $fn = 100), you get the upside-down top shown in
Figure 7.17.

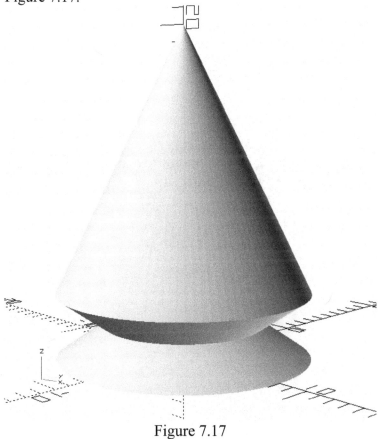

Figure 7.17

One parameter used in the 2D polygons,
linear_extrude, and rotate_extrude that I have not
mentioned is convexity. This seems to be a rather
unimportant parameter, since it does not actually affect the
rendering but may, in some rare cases, cause the preview
picture to appear be missing parts of the model. If your
preview does not look like you expect, adding convexity =
10 to the parameters in these three commands may clear up
the problem.

You can combine 2D shapes before you extrude them with either linear_extrude or rotate_extrude. For example, you can extrude a union of several shapes. For example, take the code

```
rotate_extrude()
union(){
   translate([0, 0])square([20, 40]);
   translate([0, 40])square([40, 20]);

}
```

The union of these two squares creates the shape shown in Figure 7.18, and the rotate_extrude of this creates the 3D shape shown in Figure 7.19.

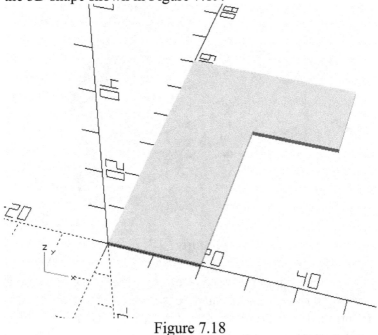

Figure 7.18

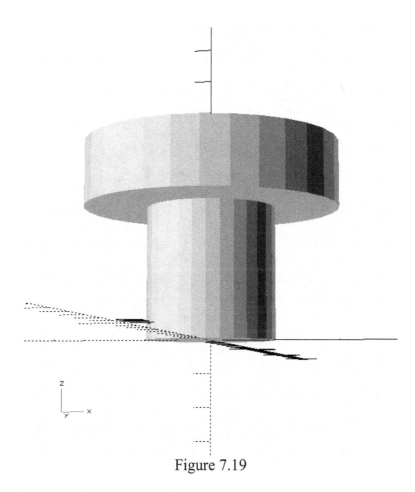

Figure 7.19

This will work for other combining methods, such as difference or intersection, as well. For example, you could get the structure in Figure 7.20 with this code.

```
difference(){
    square(15, center = true);
    circle(5, $fn = 99);
}
```

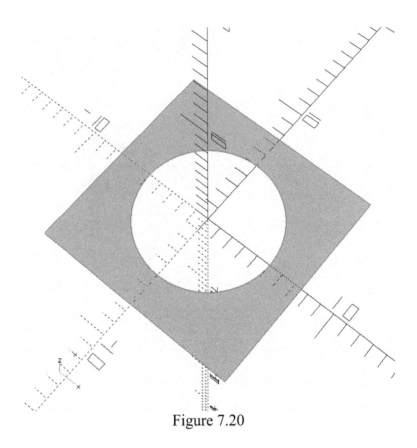

Figure 7.20

There is an additional way of combining 2D shapes called the hull. This command connects all the points of all the shapes listed as parameters. It is as if you stretched a rubber band around all the parts and then filled in all the space within the rubber band. Suppose you use the following code.

```
translate([5, 0]) circle(5);
translate([5, 40]) circle(5);
translate([45, 0]) circle(5);
```

That would produce the circles shown in Figure 7.21.

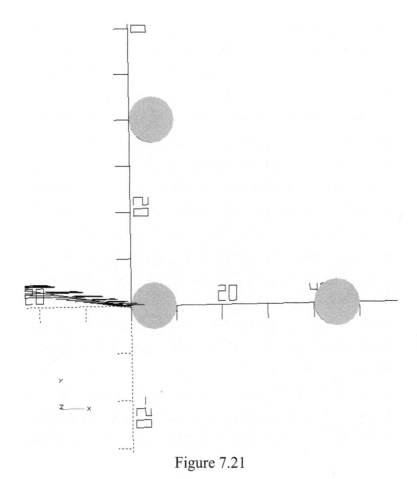

Figure 7.21

If you enclose them in a hull command like this, you get the 2D image shown in Figure 7.22.

```
hull(){
    translate([5, 0]) circle(5);
    translate([5, 40]) circle(5);
    translate([45, 0]) circle(5);
}
```

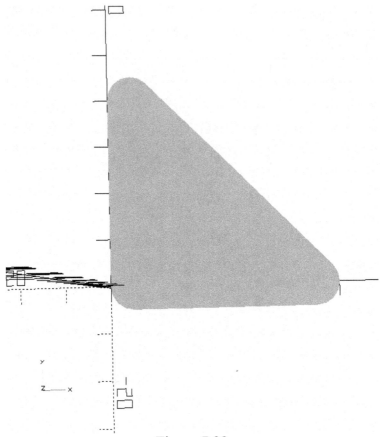

Figure 7.22

You can then linear or rotate extrude this shape or any shape made using hull. Remember, however, the requirement for rotate_extrude that all points of the figure must be on one side or the other of the Y-axis. This is why I translated the circles 5 mm in my code example.

The hull command is particularly useful in creating rounded edges for objects. Making the triangle in Figure 7.22 would have been very difficult to do by simply combining shapes. The hull command is also convenient in that you do not have to fill in all the points inside the figure.

There is another way to get just about any shape, at least any shape you can draw. You can draw a 2D shape

with certain drawing programs and save them to a file, then import this file into OpenSCAD and use this shape as your 2D image to linear_extrude or rotate_extrude. You import the picture with the import command, such as
import("sub.svg");
This gives you Figure 7.23.

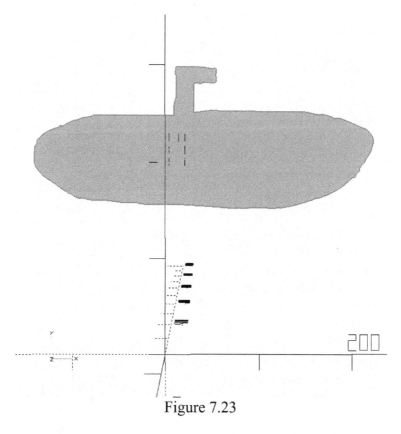

Figure 7.23

If you do not specify a file location, the OpenSCAD will look for the file in the default folder, which is the folder you have most recently saved your OpenSCAD file to. You can specify a full path, such as
import("c:/temp/sub.svg", center = true);
The location of the shape in OpenSCAD will depend on where it is in the image file you import. For example, if the shape is near the top of the image file, the

image will be farther in the Y direction. Because this can be rather unpredictable, it is generally a good idea to center the image with the center parameter, such as

import("sub.svg", center = true);

You can then extrude this just like any shape. An example of this is

linear_extrude(height = 50)
import("c:/temp/sub.svg");

Notice that if you include slashes, they must be forward slashes instead of the backslashes normally used in windows. You can use the full range of extrude options on these pictures, like scale, twist, number of degrees in rotate_extrude, etc.

This does have some limitations to importing files, however. The file must be saved in the DXF or SVG format, and there are a limited number of programs that can save in these formats. In addition, there are many variations of these formats and not all of them work. What happens if the file is not in precisely the right format is that nothing appears when you import the file and try to render it. After some experimenting, I have found that the easiest way to get a workable graphic file is to use the free program Inkscape. You can obtain this by going to https://inkscape.org/, hovering your mouse over DOWNLOAD near the top of the page, and then clicking on the "All platforms" button and then selecting download link for your platform, such as Windows:64-bit:exe.

Once you have downloaded, installed, and run Inkscape, you can draw your figure. You can ignore the box in the middle of the drawing screen. You do not need to stay inside this box. In fact, I have not been able to find any purpose to this box at all.

The easiest way to draw a figure is to use the Draw Freehand Lines tool, which looks like a pencil. Just click on this icon and then draw your shape. Be sure to come back to your starting point. This is not hard, because a small square appears at your starting point and this square turns red when you return to it. If you use this tool, you do not need to fill in the inside of your figure. OpenSCAD seems to interpret this as a solid object as long as you connect the start point and end point. You can also use the other tools, Such as the circle and rectangle tools. You can use other tools, like the Create Diagram Connector tool to draw straight lines, but in some cases you will need to use the fill tool (looks like a paint can spilling) to fill in the shape if you want OpenSCAD to treat the figure as a filled in solid object. I will not go into too much detail here, since this is a book about OpenSCAD, not Inkscape. If you want to use Inkscape to draw unique shapes, I will leave it to you to experiment. The only thing I will add is that you must save the file in SVG format. This is not a problem, since this is the default format when you press Ctrl-S or select Save under the File menu.

Chapter 8

Making 3D Models from Pictures

In the previous chapter, I discussed ways to create 3D models from 2D shapes, including SVG picture files. There is also another way to actually create 3D shapes from pictures that has some advantages and some disadvantages compared to the import command.

The other command is surface, and the simplest format is

surface(file = "filepath");

where filepath can be just a file name like "MyPicture.png" or a full path like "c:/temp/MyPicture.png". Notice that if you include slashes, they must be forward slashes instead of the backslashes normally used in windows. If no path is specified, the path used is the Windows folder where you last saved the OpenSCAD code for your project. Because of this, it is best to write at least part of the code for your project, save it, note where it was saved, and put the picture file there. Personally, I find it more convenient to create a folder off the root directory called temp (C:\temp) and put the pictures there, remembering to use forward slashes when I address the folder in OpenSCAD.

The picture must be a PNG file. If you want to work with a file that is not a PNG file, you must load the file into a graphics program and then save it as a PNG file. The file also should be small. Too large an image can slow down the rendering so much that it seems to actually lock up the computer. I recommend no larger than 100 pixels by 100 pixels, and certainly no larger than 22 X 200 mm. If you want to work with an existing picture, you need to reduce the size. I recommend the free windows Paint program for these functions. You can load in a wide range of file types (JPEG, GIF, etc.) and save them as PNG. In addition, you can use the Properties option under the File menu to see how big the picture is (be sure to set the units to pixels). If it is too big, you can use the resize function on the Home tab to shrink it. The resize function will ask for the percent of the original size that you want the new size to be. For example, if the picture is 1000 by 800 pixels, select 10% as the Resize value so no side of the picture is over 100 pixels.

The 3D structure will normally have high points where the picture is lightest and low points where the picture is darkest. That is, it extends the image upward like linear_extrude based on the brightness of the image. If you use the picture shown in Figure 8.1 which I call Steps.png and the code

surface(file = "Steps.png");

you get the structure shown in Figure 8.2.

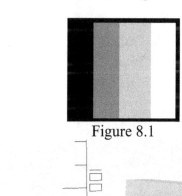

Figure 8.1

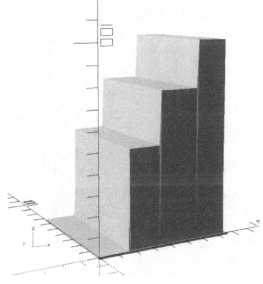

Figure 8.2

You can see how the darker the point on the picture is, the lower the point is on the 3D image. Note that even for a black spot, there is still a small amount of height. This can be a bit of a problem, which we will get into shortly. The structure is 100 mm high. The tallest point on the structure is always 100 mm high, no matter how dark or light it is. That is, it automatically adjusts to be 100 mm high. The length and width of the 3D structure will be 1 mm for every pixel in length and width of the image file.

Let's take another graphic to illustrate a point. The picture in Figure 8.3 generates the structure in Figure 8.4.

Figure 8.3

Figure 8.4

You can see again that the lighter parts of the picture are extended up. Suppose, however, you wanted it to be the other way around, with the darker parts of the image to be taller. There is a parameter for this, the invert = true parameter. The command would be
surface(file = "Face.png", invert = true);
This would give the structure in Figure 8.5.

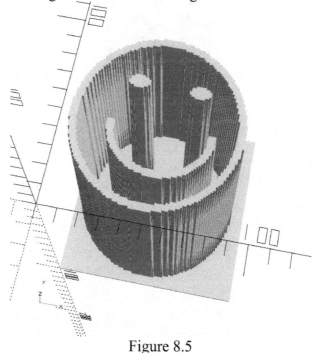

Figure 8.5

Instead of extruding the light areas up, it pushed them down. In fact, the structure is now below the X-Y plane. Again, it is 100 mm tall, but with the base 100 mm below the X-Y plane. To avoid having your 3D printer try to print below the print bed (If your slicer does not adjust the height to put the model on the bed), you can use the translate command to raise the structure 100 mm.

There is more you can do with the structure generated by the PNG image. You can take a slice of the structure to only get what you want. Consider the public domain image in Figure 8.6.

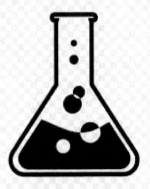

Figure 8.6

This has a checkered gray background that you probably would not want. Using the code
surface(file = "flask.png", invert = true);
you get the structure in Figure 8.7.

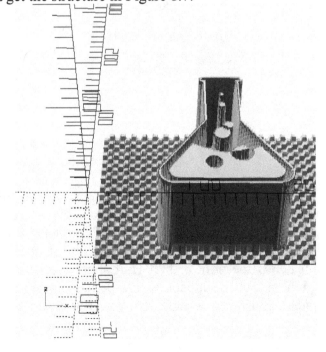

Figure 8.7

You can see the bumpy surface at the bottom created by the gray and white squares in the picture. You can slice away only what you want using the intersection() function, while at the same time raising the structure above the X-Y plane using code like this.

```
intersection(){
    translate([0, 0, 50])
    surface(file ="flask.png", invert = true);
    translate([-1, -1, 0])
    cube([400, 400, 10]);
}
```

Translating the structure created by surface up 50 mm puts the top 50 mm of it above the X-Y plane. Intersecting that with a cube that is only 10 mm high cuts out and uses only the lowest 10 mm of this structure above the X-Y plane. Note that this cube is much larger than the flask structure in the X and Y direction and has been translated –1 mm in these directions to make sure that it extends past the structure in all X and Y directions. Thus, only the part of the structure from 50 mm to 60 mm is kept. This is shown in figure 8.8.

Figure 8.8

I said that I recommend using a picture that is about 100 pixels square. If this is too large or small, you can scale the structure created. For example, you can use the code

```
scale({5, 5, 1])
intersection(){
    translate([0, 0, 50])
    surface(file = "flask.png", invert = true);
    translate([-1, -1, 0])
    cube([400, 400, 10]);
}
```

to increase the size of the flask image just created. Unfortunately, there is not a lot more you can do with the surface command. Unlike linear_extrude, surface does not have a lot of functions like twist or scale that let you manipulate the structure as it rises from the picture.

There is one other parameter you can add to the surface command. That is the center = true parameter, such as

```
surface(file = "flask.png", invert = true, center = true);
```

This causes the structure to be centered on the XY plane at the origin. It does not, however, move the structure up or down in the Z direction.

Chapter 9

Making 3D Models from Text Files

There is another way to control the structure created from the surface command. Instead of a picture, you can use a file containing a matrix of numbers, a series of rows of numbers where the numbers in a row are separated by a space. The numbers can be integers or non-integers. A typical matrix might look like this

```
0 0 0 0 0 0 3 0 0 0 0
0 0 0 0 0 0 0 0 0 0 0
0 0 0 0 0 0 0 0 0 0 0
0 0 0 2 2 0 0 0 0 0 0
0 0 0 2 2 0 0 0 0 0 0
0 0 0 0 0 0 0 0 0 0 0
0 0 0 0 0 1 2 3 2 1 0
0 0 1 0 0 1 2 3 2 1 0
0 0 0 0 0 0 0 0 0 0 0
0 0 0 0 0 0 0 0 0 0 0
```
Listing 9.1

If you saved this to a file called surface.txt in the current default OpenSCAD folder and ran the following code in OpenSCAD, you would get the shape in Figure 9.1.

```
surface(file = "surface.txt");
```

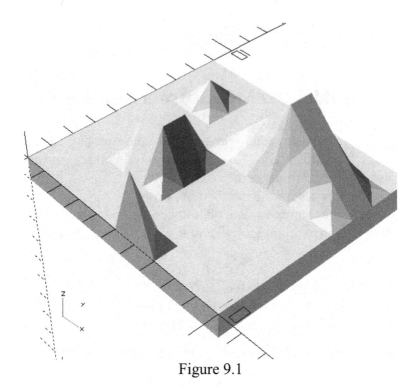

Figure 9.1

The X and Y size is one mm less than the number of numbers in the matrix. The matrix in this example is 11 numbers wide (11 columns) and 10 numbers high (10 rows), so the image is 10 mm in the X direction and 9 mm in the Y direction.

There is a 1-mm high base that extends down 1 mm below the X-Y plane. You can eliminate this is you want by using the difference function with a large cube that has the top at $Z = 0$ or by using the intersection function with a large cube that has its bottom at $Z = 0$, as we have mentioned in other chapters.

The height of each point above the X-Y plane is equal to the value of the number, and the X-Y position of the point is defined by the number's location in the matrix. For example, the single peak 1 mm high in the far corner of Figure 8.10 is caused by the number 1 in column 3, row 8 of the matrix. The numbers around that 1 in the matrix are all 0s, so the position of all those points have a Z value of

0. Notice the rather bizarre shape of the sloping sides that transition from 1 down to 0. The higher spike at X=6, Y=0 is the 3 in row 1, column 7 of the matrix. Note that the one side at the edge goes straight down because it is on the edge of the shape. This is the only way to get the edge of a point to go straight down using this technique, although I will get to a way to approximate it shortly.

You can get a flat top by putting the same value together in the matrix. You can see the shape in Figure 9.1 that has a flat top created by the four 2's together in the matrix. It still has the odd shaped sides, however.

Notice the shape in the right corner with the straight ramp up each side. This was made by having the consecutive numbers 0 1 2 3 2 1 0 in the matrix. Each of these points is then connected to the point next to it. This same sequence is repeated in the next row, so these points are connected to those points and you get a 1-mm wide shape with sloping sides.

As mentioned before, if you want the sides to go straight down, the numbers have to be at the edge of the matrix. For example, the matrix

0 6 0
0 6 0
Listing 9.2

gives you the shape in Figure 9.2.

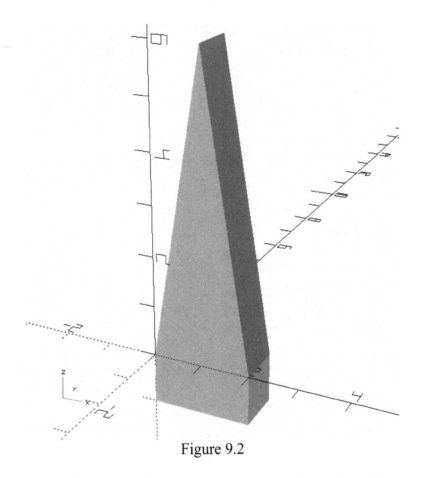

Figure 9.2

I mentioned a way to approximate the straight edge. This could be done by having a very large number of numbers in the matrix. The shape in Figure 10.3 comes from having a matrix 110 by 110 numbers. The middle 100 numbers are 100 and the 5 numbers on the border are 0. This gives you a structure of 109 mm by 109 mm (counting the base below the X-Y plain). The raised part is 100 mm square and the sloping part is only 1 mm, so it is barely perceptible. Of course, this for illustration purposes only. You would not use such a complex method to make such a simple shape when a simple cube command would work.

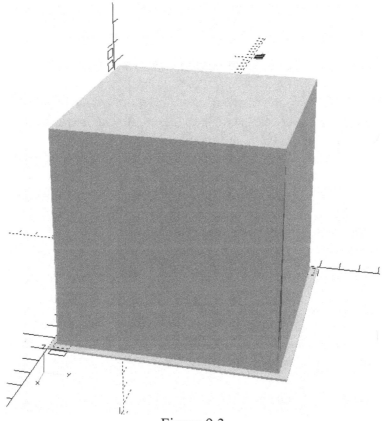

Figure 9.3

You can use the same techniques discussed in Chapter 8 to trim off the base. The part of the shape created by 0's extends 1 mm below the XY plane, so you can just intersect the figure with a large cube sitting on the XY plane to remove this part.

Frankly, I would find I much easier to just draw the shapes and make the surface from a picture using the techniques in Chapter 8, but I am including this technique in this book for the sake of completeness.

Chapter 10

Duplicating Objects

There are many occasions where you will want to make many of the same part of an object, such as teeth around a gear. There are many tools in OpenSCAD to help you do this. These tools range for making a few identical items, to making a virtually unlimited number of the same thing, to making mirror images of parts, and even bringing in STL files already created and using them to duplicate a part created with a different program.

module

The first and simplest technique is the module. A module is somewhat like a union, except that you can give it a name and then call up that code from different places in you code. The code for creating a module is

```
module PartName() {
    part 1
    part 2
    etc.
}
```

PartName can be any name you give the part, such as gear, wheel, or whatever. The parts within the curly parentheses can be any of the usual code, such as sphere, cube, etc. There can be as many or as few as you want. They can be rotated, stretched, or any other procedure you would normally use. Let's take a simple example. Put in the following code.

```
module House(){
    translate([-10,-10,0]) cube(20);
    translate([-10,-10,20]) rotate([0,45,0])
```

```
    cube([14.1,20,14.1]);
    translate([-2,8,0])cube([4,2,35]);
}
```

Listing 10.1

Press the F5 key to view it. And ……..
Absolutely nothing appears. Why? Because although you
have defined the module House, you have not actually
called for it to be generated. To actually display the House,
you need to add a line like
House();
to your code. If you add that to your code in Listing 10.1,
you get Figure 10.1.

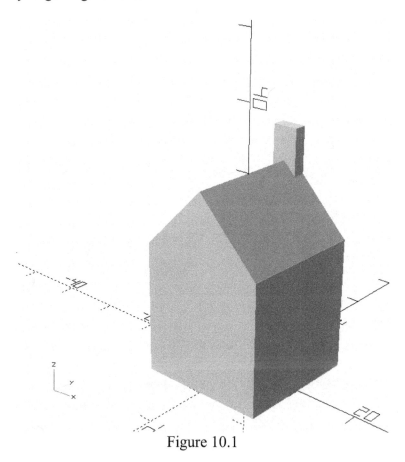

Figure 10.1

So, what was the point of this? You could have gotten the same image with just the code

```
translate([-10,-10,0]) cube(20);
translate([-10,-10,20]) rotate([0,45,0]) cube([14.1,20,14.1]);
translate([-2, 8, 0]) cube([4, 2, 35]);
```

The point is that now that you have defined the module House, you can make multiple houses, and manipulate them individually. For example, suppose you have the code in Listing 10.2.

```
module House(){
    translate([-10,-10,0])
    cube(20);
    translate([-10,-10,20])
    rotate([0,45,0])
    cube([14.1,20,14.1]);
    translate([-2,8,0])
    cube([4,2,35]);
}
House();
translate([40,0,0])
House();
translate([-0,-40,0])
rotate([0,0,180])
House();
translate([-40,-40,0])
rotate([0,0,180])scale([1,1,2])
House();
```
Listing 10.2

You then get the image in Figure 10.2.

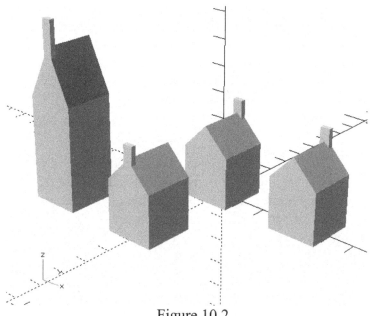

Figure 10.2

You can see that if you have some fairly complex part that appears in various forms in your total model, being able define them once and then simply call that part by a name you have assigned it can save you a lot of work. Not only do you save yourself the trouble of typing the code over and over, you also save yourself the trouble of modifying each component of the part. For example, you will obviously need to translate, rotate, or otherwise change the component when you put multiple copies of it in your project. With a module, you need only apply the command to the defined module and it applies to each component, rather than figuring out how to apply it to each component individually.

You can also modify each copy of a module by including parameters inside the parenthesis after the module name. You give each parameter a name (which can be as simple as a single letter or a longer name) and refer to this name within the module definition. Take the module in Listing 10.3, for example.

```
module House(Height, Width){
    translate([-10, 0, 0]) cube([20, Width, Height]);
    translate([-10, 0, Height]) rotate([0, 45, 0])
    cube([14.1, Width, 14.1]);
    translate([-2, Width, 0]) cube([4, 2, Height + 20]);
}
```

Listing 10.3

Now when you use the House module, you can (in fact, must) include two numbers that define how tall and wide the house is. For example, you could say House(20,30); for a wide one-story house or House(40,20); for a narrow, two-story house. This way, if you are making a model like the one in Figure 10.2, you can make your variations within the module name, which can be simpler than including a lot of scale commands in your code. You could even include the parameters for the translation or rotation in the module parameter list, like House(Height, Width, Rot, XLocation, YLocation) and then include rotate and translate commands inside the module code.

As I said, the names of the parameters can be anything, but it helps you to keep track of what they are as you develop your model if you give them descriptive names. Be sure not to give them names that are used by OpenSCAD itself. For example, you may recall that the shape cylinder has parameters h, r, and d, such as cylinder(h = 3, r = 1). Therefore, you must not use h, r, or d as your own parameter names, or you will get an error message and the model will not compile properly. Likewise, you could not use rotate, translate, or other words already defined within OpenSCAD as parameter names.

mirror

For some symmetric projects, you may need a mirror image of a part, rather than an exact duplicate of the part. For some parts, you can reverse the part simply by rotating it. However, for some complex parts, there is no way you can create an exact symmetric opposite of the part just by rotating it. Take, for example, the structure in Figure 10.3.

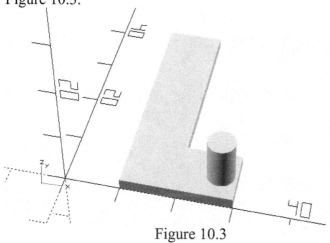

Figure 10.3

If you wanted that on both sides of your model, there is no way you can simply rotate it to make a symmetric copy of it. This is where the mirror command comes in handy. You almost always apply the mirror command to a module that you have created. The format for the mirror command is mirror([X,Y,Z]). You will almost always put a 0 in two of those positions and a 1 in one of them, such as mirror([1,0,0]). The object you apply the mirror command to is reversed or mirrored in the direction of the parameter where you inserted the non-zero value. Let's take the object in Figure 10.3 as an example. This was created with the code

```
module Bracket(){
    cube([10,40,2]);
    cube([20,10,2]);
    translate([17,5,0]) cylinder(h = 10, d = 5, $fn = 99);
}
translate([10,0,0]) Bracket();
```

Listing 10.4

97

Here we have created a module called Bracket and translated it 10 mm. Now to add a symmetrical reverse of this, we just add
translate([-10, 0, 0]) mirror([1, 0, 0]) Bracket();
to the end of Listing 10.4. This gives up the structure shown in Figure 10.4.

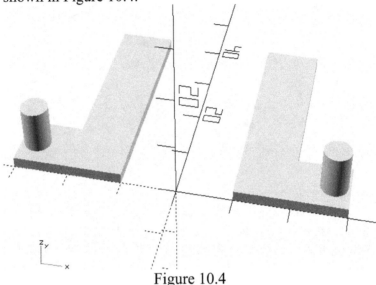

Figure 10.4

It is interesting to note that you get the same structure if you had instead added the line
mirror([1, 0, 0]) translate([10, 0, 0]) Bracket();
because you are mirroring the translation along with the Bracket. In fact, you can build the translation into the module itself and then create both object and its mirror image without another mention of the translation, like this:

```
module Bracket(){
    translate([10, 0, 0]){
        cube([10, 40, 2]);
        cube([20, 10, 2]);
        translate([17, 5, 0]) cylinder(h = 10, d = 5, $fn = 99);
    } // End translation
} // End module
Bracket();
```

mirror([1, 0, 0]) Bracket();
Listing 10.5

This only really works well if you only want one mirror image, but it can be very useful. I often create a model that is symmetric and has a complex component on each side. I can create the central part of the model, then build the complex component on one side as a module. I tweak it until I get everything, including placement, just right on one side of the model, then simply add a mirror of the component and I have the matching component on the other side.

I would like to point out again that you can mirror the object in any direction, not just the X direction. If the last line of Listing 10.5 had read
mirror([0,1,0])Bracket();
instead, you would have gotten the structure in Figure 10.5.

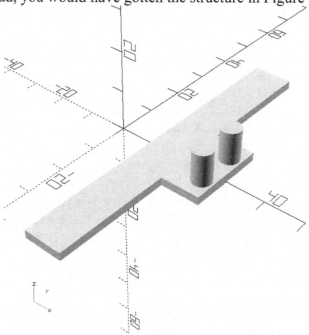

Figure 10.5

You can also mirror the object in two or even all three directions at once, although when you get to three you start getting weird results. I have personally never had a reason to mirror an object in more than one direction. Just for fun, you might take the code in Listing 10.5 and play around with trying various directions and combinations of directions for your mirroring. I will also mention, just to save you the trouble of experimenting, that it does not make any difference what number (other than 0) that you put in any of the three places in the mirror command. I have used 1 simply because it is the simplest, but it could be 3 or 10 or even a negative number. The non-zero number simply is a marker to tell OpenSCAD to mirror the object in that direction.

for

A very useful tool for creating a LOT of some component is the for operator. It is called an operator because it operates on objects. In its most common form, it takes one variable name and three numbers in the format for (X = [n1 : n2 : n3]) where n1, n2, and n3 and usually specific numbers (although they can be defined constants or even variables) and X can be any variable name. Note the use of colons rather than the usual commas to separate the numbers.

The commands and shapes that follow the for operator are duplicated multiple times determined by the values of n1, n2, and n3. The variable name used in the for operator can be used as parameters in the commands and shapes that follow the for operator. The number n1 is the starting value of the variable, n2 is the amount to increment the variable by, and n3 is the upper limit of how high (or low if n2 is negative) the variable can go. This sounds rather complex, so let's just take a simple example. Suppose we say
for(X = [0 : 10 : 50]) translate([X, 0, 0]) sphere(5);

Note that X is starting at 0, increasing by 10, and has an upper limit of 50, so X will have the values 0, 10, 20, 30, 40, and 50. The result of this is shown in Figure 10.6.

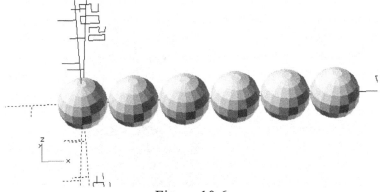

Figure 10.6

You can see that this created six spheres and translated each one a distance determined by the value of X at the time that sphere was created. The value of the variable can be used several times in the commands that follow the for operator, such as the commands
for(X = [10:10:50]) translate([X,0,0]) cube([10,10, 2 * X]);
which creates the structure shown in Figure 10.7.

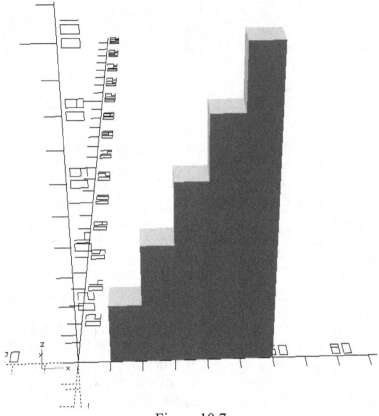

Figure 10.7

Here the value of X not only determined the position of the cube, but also the height. The value of the variable will almost certainly be used to alter the location of the objects created in some way, since there is no point in creating multiple copies of an object in exactly the same place. However, it does not have to be a translation. Another example is to use the value of the variable to set a rotation, such as

for (X = [0 : 20 : 340]) rotate([0,0,X])
translate([10, 0, 0]) cylinder(h = 2, r = 5, $fn = 3);

Here we create a triangle by making a cylinder with three sides ($fn = 3), translate it 10 mm from the Z-axis, and then use the for operator to create 18 of them rotated from 0 to 340 degrees. The result is the gear shown in Figure 10.8.

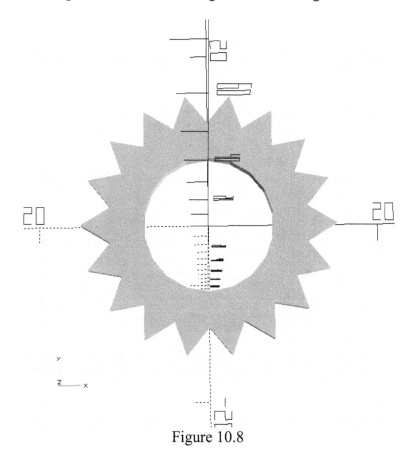

Figure 10.8

You can follow the for operator with multiple separate objects by using the {} brackets, for example

```
for (X = [0 : 20 : 80]){
    translate([X, 0, 0]) cylinder(h = 10, r = 5);
    translate([X, 0, 10]) sphere(5);
}
```

The for operators can be nested, meaning one can be inside another as long as they use different variable names. Consider the code in Listing 10.6, which creates the structures in Figure 10.9. Note that there is one { for each for and then one } for each at the end.

```
for (X = [0 : 20 : 80]){
    for(Y = [20 : 20 : 100]){
        translate([X,Y,0]) cylinder(h = 10, r1 = 5, r2 = 0);
    }
}
```

Listing 10.6

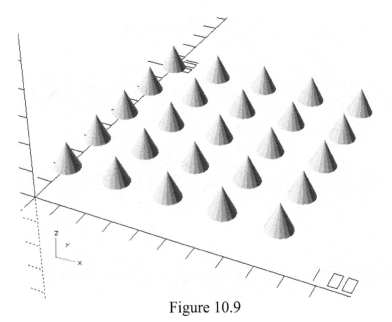

Figure 10.9

You can, incidentally, use the first variable in the second for operator. For example, the second line of Listing 10.6 could have been

for (Y = [20 : 20 : X]){

That would give you the model shown in Figure 10.10.

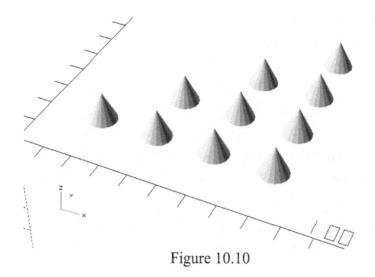

Figure 10.10

In the vast majority of cases, you will want the objects to be spaced and/or altered in a steady progression and use the for operator as described above. However, in the unusual case that you want to place or alter the shape in an irregular pattern, you can instead list the values of the variable separated by commas (not colons). For example,
for (X =[1, 5, 17, 10]) translate([X, 0, 0]) sphere(d = 3, $fn = 99);
will place spheres of diameter 3 at X locations 1, 5, 17, and 10. Note that the numbers do not have to be in any particular order.

importing 3D graphic files

If you have an STL, OFF, AMF, or 3MF file, either one you created yourself or one you downloaded, you can import it into your model. Once there, you can perform many of the normal operations like adding to it, removing sections, scaling it, etc. This is generally useful if you find a file that you like but want to modify. The format for the command is
import("FilePathAndName");
Typical examples are
import("robot.stl");

and
```
import("c:/temp/robot.stl");
```
If the file you are importing is in the same folder as you are storing your SCAD files, you do not need to specify a path. Otherwise, you must specify the path and be sure to use forward slashes rather then the usual back slashes in your folder description.

You can import more than one file. This could allow you to merge or combine several files you have found. It can also be a way to repeat the component by saving it as an STL files and then repeatedly importing it. This can also be a timesaver for you if you have created a very complex component that takes a very long time to render from the OpenSCAD code. You can render it once and save the STL file, then import it into a model that includes that component. Basically, you are using the STL file much as you used a module.

You can add the convexity parameter to the import command, such as
```
import("robot.stl", convexity = 10);
```
As before, this merely affects the appearance when previewing and I have never actually found a case where it was needed at all. I mention it here only for the sake of completeness.

include

If you have written code that includes modules and saved it to a file, you can include that code in your model without actually typing it in by using the include command at the beginning of your code. This is in the form
```
include <filename>;
```
A typical example would be
```
include <myparts.scad>;
```
OpenSCAD automatically adds the scad file extension, so be sure to include that in the file name. You must also be sure that the file contains only the module definitions, not the actual call to the module. If your file

actually calls the module, the module will actually appear in your model, and you probably not want it there. Let's take an example. Suppose you write the following code and save it in a file named Wheel.scad.

```
Size = 10;
module Wheel(){
    cylinder(h = 2, r = Size, $fn = 99);
    cylinder(h = 20, r = 2, $fn = 99);
}
```

Listing 10.7

If you put
include <Wheel.scad>
at the beginning of your code, you can then put something like
translate([10, 0, Size]) rotate([90, 0, 0]) Wheel();
in your and the wheel will appear. Note everything in your Wheel.scad file is included in your new file, including the constant definitions. This is why you must not have a call to the modules in your original file. If you had Wheel(); in your Wheel.scad file, then that wheel would have appeared in your new model, most likely in a place you do not want it, and you cannot move that copy of the wheel because the information on its translation, rotation, etc. is in the original file. It is therefore helpful to you to create files containing just module definitions for useful parts you have created and include them in your future models. The effect is the same as if you had simply copied and pasted the code from the old file, but your new file will appear less cluttered.

One more comment on this. Putting just the name of the scad file in the <> marks assumes that the old file is in the same folder as you are saving the new file in. This is most likely, but if for some reason you are saving the new file in a different folder, you will need to include the full file path.

Chapter 11

Math Functions

OpenSCAD comes will a selection of math function that you can use to automatically calculate values for some of the parameters in your commands. These can be particularly useful within for loops where you want to have a value, such as height, change in a specific way depending on location or other factors, although they are sometimes convenient in single instances. There are 24 functions, but many of them are very complex mathematical concepts and have little use in most modeling, so I will only discuss a few of the more useful ones.

sqrt

The sqrt function gives the square root of a number. The format is sqrt(n). For example, suppose you wanted to make the house shown in Figure 11.1.

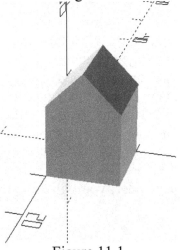

Figure 11.1

You can do that by creating one cube, then creating another cube, rotating it -45 degrees along the X-axis, and moving it up by the size of the first cube. However, the size of the second cube along the Y and Z directions must be the size of the first cube divided by the square root of 2, as shown by the code in Listing 11.1.

```
Size = 10;
cube(Size);
translate([0,0,size]) rotate([-45, 0, 0])
cube([Size, Size / sqrt(2), Size / sqrt(2)]);
```
Listing 11.1

sin

The sin function gives you the sine of an angle. The format is sin(N). You can use that, for example, to make a wavy shape such as shown in Figure 11.2 by using the code in Listing 11.2.

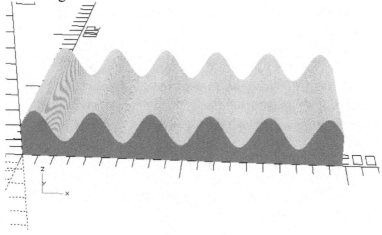

Figure 11.2

```
repeats = 5.5;
for (A = [0 : 1 : 360 * repeats]){
    translate([A * .1, 0, 0]) cube([.1, 100, (2 + sin(A)) * 10]);
}
```
Listing 11.2

109

Here we are making cubes (2 + sin(A)) * 10 high and .1 mm wide, and translating then by distance A. Thus, as A increases, each block is moved a little bit (0.1 mm) which is also the width of each block, so each block is right next to the last one. The height of each one goes up and down in a sine wave as the angle A increases. Multiplying by 10 is just to make the ripples more pronounced, and the addition of the 2 is to make sure that the height never goes negative, since the sine function does and height of a cube cannot be negative. I could have used 1 instead of 2, but that would mean zero height in some places. The variable repeats is just the number of times you want to go through the cycle, and therefore the number of ripples.

This is one example of using math functions to shape your models. Many of the following can be used in a similar fashion to generate shapes using a for loop and small cubes or other shapes that are changed based on the math function.

cos

The cos function gives you the cosine of an angle, which is really just the sine of the angle plus 90. I do not see a lot of reason to use both, but I am including it for completeness. The format is cos(A)

tan

The tan function gives you the tangent of an angle. The format is tan(A).

asin

The asin function gives you the arcsine (inverse sine) of a number. That is, it gives you the angle that would generate that number if you took the sine of that angle. The format is asin(N).

acos

The acos function gives you the arccosine (inverse cosine) of a number if you took the cosine of that angle. That is, it gives you the angle that would generate that number. The format is acos(N).

atan

The atan function gives you the arctangent (inverse tangent) of a number if you took the tangent of that angle. That is, it gives you the angle that would generate that number. The format is atan(N). I will use this in an example in the projects section of this book.

ln

The ln function gives you the natural log of a number. The format is ln(N).

log

The log function gives you the base 10 log of a number. The format is log(N).

pow

The pow function takes two parameters, and it raises the first parameter to the power of the second. For example, pow(10, 3) gives you $10 \wedge 3$, which is 1000.

rands

The function rands is a random number generator. It generates a list of random numbers. It takes three parameters, with an optional fourth parameter. The first is the minimum value of the random numbers. The second is the maximum value of the random numbers. The third is the number of random numbers to generate. The format is variable = rands(N1, N2, N3);

The numbers are stored in the variable as a list.

For example,

X = rands(0, 10, 5);

This generates 5 random numbers from 0 to 10. The random numbers are stored in X in the format X[0], X[1], X[2], X[3], and X[4]. That is, you access each random number by calling for the variable name followed by a number enclosed in square brackets. Note that the numbers start at 0, not 1.

You can use this feature to generate irregular shapes. Take, for example, the code

```
X = rands(0, 10, 100);
Y = rands(0,10,100);
S = rands(.5, 2, 100);
for (N = [0 : 99]){
    translate([X[N], Y[N], 0]) sphere(S[N], $fn = 99);
}
```

This generates 100 values for X, Y, and S. Using these to set the X and Y locations (through the translate command) and the sphere size, an image like the one in Figure 11.3 is generated.

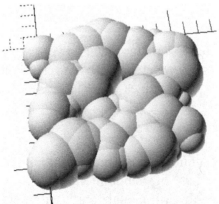

Figure 11.3

This is, of course, just an example. The point is that you can use rands to randomly generate values for the location, size, scaling, etc. of objects in cases where you want to create random objects, such as a hilly landscape or large numbers of randomly placed objects like trees in a forest.

The actual model generated will be different each time you generate it by pressing F5 or F6. This can be very frustrating if you generate a shape you like, and then cannot get it back again as you construct the rest of your model. There is a way around this. I mentioned that there is an optional fourth parameter to rands. You can use the format variable = rands(N1, N2, N3, N4);

The fourth number is called a seed value, and it controls the generation of the random numbers. If you put in a specific number for this forth value, such as 10, the string of random numbers generated will always be the same. You can experiment with using different numbers for the seed number and if you get a shape you like, keep that number as you work on the rest of the model you are building.

floor

The floor function returns the largest integer number that is not larger than the parameter. The format is floor(N). For example, floor(2.35) returns a value of 2. One use for this is in combination with the rands function described above. The rands function generates non-integer numbers like 3.25387, sometimes called floating point numbers. If you want to have integer random numbers, generate the numbers using rands and then use floor like floor(X[0]) to convert it to an integer.

round

The round function is similar to the floor function, except that it rounds to the nearest number, not always down. For example, floor(4.6) gives 4, while round(4.6) gives 5. Its possible uses are the same as floor.

Additional mathematical operations

There are additional mathematical operations available in OpenSCAD, but these are extremely complicated to use, and I have found not use for them in modeling. I believe that they are for other application of OpenSCAD, like animation. Therefore, I will not cover the remaining math functions.

Chapter 12

Making Checking Your Coding Easier

In this chapter, I will discuss a few tips and techniques for making it easier to develop, debug, test and alter your models. These tips are designed to make it easier for you to keep track of what is happening in your models as they become more complex.

Check your model after each addition

This is very simple, but it pays to render you model after you add each part. Hit the F5 key after you add each line. For one thing, if you have made a mistake in the typing, you will get your error message immediately and can quickly identify what went wrong. For another, if the new part is wrong, like you have misjudged the size you want, you will see the mistake immediately before you waste time adding more parts that may not fit and will need to be adjusted too when you correct the incorrect piece.

Commenting

The second tip is simple and should be familiar to anyone who has done much coding. Heavily comment your code with remarks. As you have seen in some of the examples in this book, anything after a double slash (//) in a line will be ignored. This allows you to make comments that do not affect your actual model in your code to help you keep track of it. Identifying what each line in your code does as you write that line will help you identify them quickly later.

For example, you will probably have many cubes, cylinders, and other shapes in your models. If you create the model and one part, such as one cylinder, does not look right in the final model, you can find it easily.

I find it especially helpful to identify the significance of each close bracket. Take the following code for example.

```
difference(){
  union(){
    cylinder(h = 2, r = 20, $fn = 99); // Wheel
    cylinder(h = 8, r = 5, $fn = 99); //Support
  } //End union
  // Next line is Hole
  translate([0, 0, -1]) cylinder(h = 10, r = 2, $fn = 99);
  // Next line is Notch
  translate([0,-1,-1]) cube([4,2,10]);
} // End difference
```

By identifying what each part is, it makes it easy to change one later if that piece does not fit properly. By clearly marking what each } is the end of, it makes it easy to see where to insert something else it that becomes necessary later.

On a related note, it is a big help in following your code if you indent each section of code where multiple lines are enclosed in squiggly brackets. These basically form separate sections of code. For example:

```
difference(){
  union(){
    cube([20, 10, 10]);
    cube([10, 20, 5]);
  } // End union
  translate([5, 5, -1]) cylinder(h = 30, r = 3);
} // End difference
```

You can see how this makes it easy to see at a glance where sections of the code start and stop. Note: The appearance of the indenting in the OpenSCAD editor will not look exactly it does in this book. In particular, statements that wrap around more than one line may not be as evenly indented as they are in my examples in my book.

Color coding pieces

You can cause a piece, such as a cube or sphere, to be a different color by using the color parameter, which takes the form color("ColorName"). Take the following code, for example.

```
color("red") cube(5);
color("blue") cylinder(h = 10,r = 1, $fn = 99);
translate([4,0,0]) color("green") cube([2, 10, 2]);
translate([0, 0, 10]) sphere(2, $fn = 99);
```
                        Listing 12.1

This gives the image in Figure 21.1. (If you are reading this in a black and white copy of this book, you will not get the full effect of this illustration.)

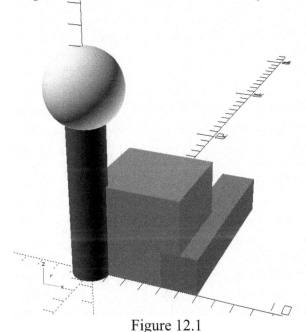

Figure 12.1

You can see that this makes it much easier to distinguish the individual pieces, including where each piece ends. You can, for example, easily see that the lower cube is actually part way inside the taller cube. If your intent had been to put that cube on the edge of the taller cube, you can see your mistake. Note that if you do not include the color command, the piece defaults to the yellow.

I want to emphasize that this does not affect your 3D model or exported STL file at all. In fact, when you press the F6 key for the actual rendering, the colors will disappear. The purpose of this color function was originally for other uses for OpenSCAD, like creating pictures, but you can use this as a diagnostic tool in developing your models.

Temporarily remove pieces from your model

Sometimes when you have created a complex model, it is hard to get a look at individual pieces. You can remove individual pieces from the model temporarily by several methods.

One way is to put a double slash (//) at the beginning of the line describing the piece. For example, in the following code, the cube will not be shown.

```
sphere(5);
//cube(8);
cylinder(h = 10, r = 2);
```

Listing 12.2

However, this can be a rather unreliable. Suppose you have put a line break in the description of the piece, such as in the following code

```
sphere(5);
translate([20, 0, 0])
```

```
cube(8);
cylinder(h = 10, r = 2);
```
                    Listing 12.3

If you put the double slash in the beginning of the translate line, only the translation is removed and the cube is still shown, but not translated. If you put a double slash in the beginning of the cube line, the translate command will be applied to the cylinder.

A better way in most cases is to put an asterisk in the beginning of the line. This tells OpenSCAD to ignore the object. In the case of Listing 12.3, putting an asterisk in the beginning of either the translate line or the cube line causes the cube to disappear without affecting any of the other pieces.

There is a situation where you might want to use the remark option to temporarily remove objects. That is where you want to remove a large number of objects. There is another type of remark marker. If you put a slash followed by an asterisk (/*) in the code and later in the code put an asterisk followed by a slash (*/), everything in between will be treated as a remark and not used. For example, in the code in Listing 12.4, all the cubes disappear.

```
sphere(5);
/*
translate([20, 0, 0]) cube(8);
translate([20, 20, 0]) cube(8);
translate([0, 20, 0]) cube(8);
*/
cylinder(h = 10,r = 2);
```
                    Listing 12.4

Making a component transparent

Instead of removing a component completely, you can make a component transparent and tinted red by putting a pound sign (#) at the beginning of the line describing it.

For example, the code in Listing 12.5 gives you the picture in Figure 12.2 when you press F5.

```
#translate([0, 0, 10]) sphere(10, $fn = 999);
translate([-10,-10,0]) cube([20, 20, 5]);
translate([0, 0,1 5]) cylinder(h = 10, r = 4, $fn = 999);
```
                         Listing 12.5

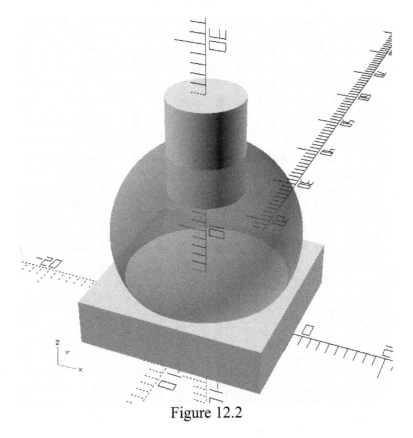

Figure 12.2

This can make it easier to see how components are fitting together without totally removing them using some of the techniques discussed previously.

120

Showing individual pieces

You can cause OpenSCAD to show only one piece by putting an exclamation point (!) at the beginning of that line. For example, in the code in Listing 12.6, only the first cube is displayed when you press F5 or F6. This makes it easy to see the shape and location of that piece.

```
sphere(5);
!translate([20, 0, 0]) cube(8);
translate([20, 20, 0]) cube(8);
translate([0, 20, 0]) cube(8);
cylinder(h = 10, r = 2);
```
                                        Listing 12.6

Finding invisible pieces

As described in Chapter 5, you can put components into your code that do not add objects to your model, but actually take away from it. These subtracting components should always intersect with the main components that they are subtracting or cutting away from. The most common example is the difference command, where everything after the first object (or union if you create one) is actually removed, not added. These components are not visible when you use the F5 or F6 keys to preview or render your model. Sometimes if the result you get does not look right because you did not place the invisible components right, you may want to see these components so you can see exactly how you have misplaced them. I did mention that you can use the thrown together function (activated by the F12 key or from the View menu) to see these invisible components. However, there is a flaw in this. If the invisible component does not insect any other component at all, they will not show up even in the Thrown Together view. This can happen if you have seriously miscalculated the placement of the subtracting component.

There is a simple technique for finding these missing components. As I mentioned above, you can put a pound sign (#) at the beginning of the line describing a component to make it transparent. This will also make the shape being cut away visible. That is, putting a # at the beginning of a line describing a shape to be cut-away will cause the invisible component to show up as a semitransparent red object, regardless of where it is. For example, look at Listing 12.7.

```
difference(){
    sphere(5, $fn = 99);
    translate([-5, -5, -10]) cube(10);
} // End difference
```
Listing 12.7

This creates the dome in Figure 12.3.

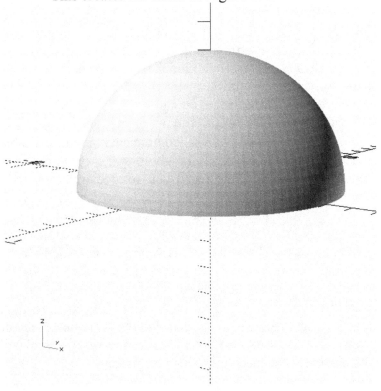

Figure 12.3

Suppose, however, you forget the minus signs in the translate command and write Listing 12.8.

```
difference(){
   sphere(5, $fn = 99);
   translate([5, 5, 10]) cube(10);
} // End difference
```
                        Listing 12.8

In this case, the sphere and cube will not intersect at all and even using Thrown Together will not show the cube. However, if you put the pound sign at the beginning of the cube line as shown in Listing 12.9, you will see both the sphere and the cube.

```
difference(){
   sphere(5, $fn = 99);
   #translate([5, 5, 10]) cube(10);
} // End difference
```
                        Listing 12.9

You can then change the translation command to maneuver the cube into the proper position while it is visible, then remove the pound sign when you have it in the proper place. Actually, it is not absolutely necessary to remove the pound sign, because it has no effect when you actually render the model with F6 to produce your final STL file.

There is one other effect of marking the component with the pound sign. I mentioned in chapter 1 that you can automatically zooms in or out to show you your entire model by clicking on the magnifying glass icon or pressing Ctrl-Shift-V. If a component is not visible, this will not zoom to include this. However, if you mark the component with the # and then press F5, when you zoom to see the entire model it will zoom to include this component, no matter where it is.

Matching opening and closing brackets

Just in case you have not remarked closing brackets as described above, this is a little trick you can use to find the proper closing bracket. If you put the typing cursor (not the mouse cursor) right after the opening bracket, both the opening and closing bracket will be highlighted in a sort of light blue. Put the typing cursor right after any bracket, then scroll down through the code until you see a closing bracket highlighted in blue. Also, you can put the typing cursor right after the closing bracket, and the opening bracket will have the highlight. This works with any type of bracket or parenthesis, including (, [, and {.

The console

The console is the area in the lower right portion of the screen. This gives a report every time you compile (preview or render) your code. It is well worth viewing after you do this. Note: Before you preview or render your code, right-click on the console window and then left-click on the word Clear and appears in the menu. This will erase everything in the console window so you know that what appears next is entirely about the latest compile.

One thing the console reports is any errors in your code that is finds when OpenSCAD compiles it. The error message is highlighted in yellow. The most common error message tells you that a line was ignored because OpenSCAD could not understand it. This means the component described in that line simply does not appear in the image you see.

The error message usually ends in a line number. This line number usually correctly indicates the line where you have a typo or other mistake, making it easy to fix it.

To make it even easier, the exact point where the mistake occurs in often shown in red in your code. However, for some errors, OpenSCAD cannot identify where the error is. For example, if you leave out a closing } symbol, OpenSCAD has no way of knowing where that symbol is supposed to be. In these cases, the error message often gives a number one more than the total number of lines in the code. In that case, you need to backtrack through your code to find the missing }.

A tool you can use in your code to make additional use of the console is the echo command. The format for this is

echo(variable);

An example in code would be

```
for (X = [1:5]){
   echo(X);
}
```

Listing 12.10

If you run this, you will see the following in the console window.

ECHO: 1
ECHO: 2
ECHO: 3
ECHO: 4
ECHO: 5

Of course, you would probably use something more complicated, like echoing the value of some more complex computation.

Cutting away parts temporarily

As described previously, the difference command can make parts of objects disappear. Normally, you use this to permanently change the shape of part of your model. However, you can use it to temporarily make parts disappear just so you can see inside more clearly. Take, for example, the following code to put a cylinder part way through a hole in a cube.

```
difference(){
    translate([-5, -5, 0]) cube(10);
    translate([0, 0, 2]) cylinder(h = 10, r = 3, $fn = 99);
} // End difference
translate([0, 0, 3]) cylinder(h = 10, r = 2.5, $fn = 99);
```
Listing 12.11

This makes the model in Figure 12.4.

Figure 12.4

You cannot really see how far the cylinder goes down or whether it touches the sides anywhere. However, you can get a look inside by making the entire structure a union, then using difference to cut away a part of it. Listing 12.12 shows how to do this, and Figure 12.5 shows the results.

```
difference(){ // temporary cut out just to see inside
    union(){
        difference(){
            translate([-5, -5, 0]) cube(10);
            translate([0, 0, 2]) cylinder(h = 10,r = 3, $fn = 99);
        } // End of difference
```

translate([0, 0, 3]) cylinder(h 10, r = 2.5, $fn = 99);
} // End of union
translate([-10, 0, -1]) cube(20); // Temporary cube
} // End temporary difference

Listing 12.12

Figure 12.5

You can see that this allows you to see inside the structure and se that the cylinder does not touch the cube at the sides or bottom, which presumably is what you want. Once you have looked inside and satisfied yourself with the design, you would remove the difference command, the closing } bracket, and the cube used to cut away the section.

Of course, this is just an example, and this structure would not print. However, it demonstrated that by uniting your entire structure into a union and then using difference to cut away parts of it, you can see inside your design to make sure it is right.

Chapter 13

Hinges

Now that we have discussed most of the basics of using OpenSCAD, we will have a series of chapters giving you specific code for possibly useful components that you can assemble into useful models. I will try to make these useful examples instructive also, demonstrating some of the techniques previously discussed. I'll let you in on a little secret. I love 3D printing things that move and can be printed in place, meaning you do not have to assemble them after you print them, so there will be a fair number of them in this book.

Let's start off with creating a hinge. This will be one way (I will discuss others in following chapters) to make models that can have moving parts.

A hinge usually has a solid shaft that goes through a series of holes. Unfortunately, it can be difficult to print some things with a 3D printer that have long overhanging parts. By overhanging parts I mean parts that go a long way with nothing supporting them. In this book, all my models will not use support structures, which means that they will have to be shaped carefully. Fortunately, you can almost always 3D print a shape with overhanging parts that slope gradually outward. I generally find an angle of at least 45 degrees quite safe to print. For example, almost any 3D printer can print the shape in Figure 13.1, because the overhang slopes up by 45 degrees.

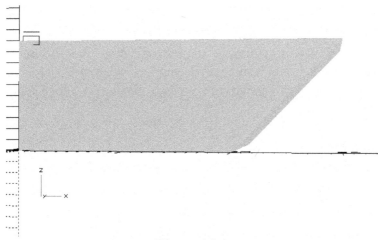

Figure 13.1

By the same principle, a cone as shown on Figure 13.2 can usually be printed.

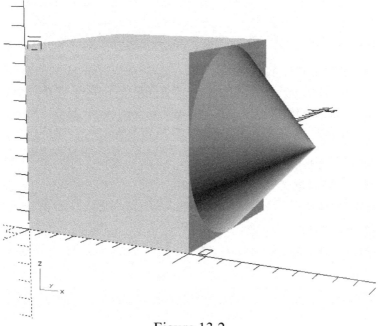

Figure 13.2

This type of cone will be used extensively in the hinge design. But first, let's design the simpler part, the holes. This is a simple matter of using the difference command to cut a hole in a support structure. Here is a simple code in Listing 13.1, which gives you the structure in Figure 13.3.

```
height = 5;
HoleSize = 3.4;
holeConnectorWidth = 2.25;
holeConnectorLength = 3.5;

module holeConnector(){
    difference(){
        union(){
            cube([holeConnectorWidth, holeConnectorLength,
            height]);
            translate([0,holeConnectorLength,height/2])
            rotate([0,90,0])
            cylinder(h = holeConnectorWidth, d = height, $fn =
            99);
        } // End union
        translate([-1, holeConnectorLength, height / 2])
        rotate([0,90,0])
        cylinder(h = holeConnectorWidth + 2, d = HoleSize,
        $fn = 99);
    }// End difference
} // End holesConnector module
```
                        Listing 13.1

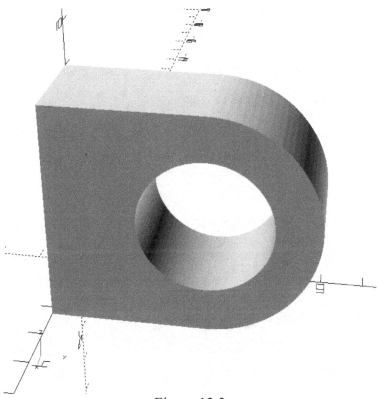

Figure 13.3

You will need at least two of these for your hinge, so we create a module that simply puts two of these side-by-side.

```
module Holes(){
    translate([6-holeConnectorWidth/2, -2.1,0])
    holeConnector();
    translate([14-holeConnectorWidth/2, -2.1,0])
    holeConnector();
} // End Holes module
```
                              Listing 13.2

This is shown in Figure 13.4.

131

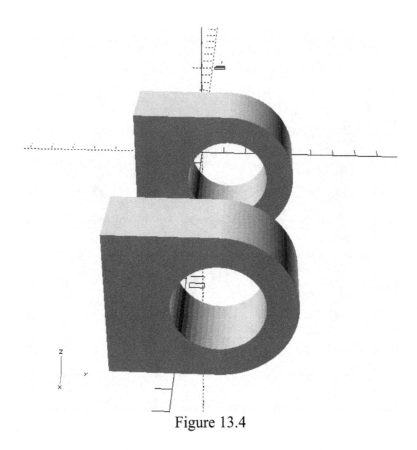

Figure 13.4

You will need to attach these to something to hold them in place and also to have something actually swing on the hinge, but for the sake of generality we will just leave these unattached for now.

The next step is what is normally a pin in a hinge. As explained above, a long unsupported structure is hard to print, and the center pin clearly cannot be touching the holes it goes through. Therefore, we will use cones as explained above. We can create the following module.

```
module cone(R,D){
    translate([D,1.35,height/2])
    rotate([0,R,0])
    cylinder(h = 2.3, r1 = 2.3, r2 = 0, $fn = 99);
} // End cone module
```

This creates a cone that can be placed along the Y axis using the D (for Distance) parameter and pointed (rotated) by the proper amount by the R parameter. You can attach these to supports. The supports can be the same shape as shown in Figure 13.3, but without the holes. This can be done using the module defined in Listing 13.3, which creates the component shown in Figure 13.5. Note that we define $fn = 99 at the beginning so we do not have to include it in each cylinder line.

```
module Pins(){
    $fn = 99;
    translate([0, 1.4, 0]) cube([4, 3.6, height]);
    translate([0, 1.4, 2.5]) rotate([0, 90, 0])
    cylinder(h = 4, d = 5);
    translate([8, 1.4, 0]) cube([4, 3.6, height]);
    translate([8,1.4,2.5]) rotate([0,90,0])
    cylinder(h = 4, d = 5);
    translate([16, 1.4, 0]) cube([4, 3.6, height]);
    translate([16, 1.4, 2.5]) rotate([0, 90, 0])
    cylinder(h = 4, d = 5);
    cone(90, 4);
    cone(-90, 8);
    cone(90, 12);
    cone(-90, 16.1);
} // End Pins module
```
Listing 3.3

Figure 13.5

133

Notice how the cones have actually merged at the points. The gradual slope of the cones allows you to print them, but you still get a solid pin. Now let's put the holes and the pin together by defining a module for the entire link.

```
module FullLink(){
   Holes();
   Pins();
}
```

This creates the model shown in Figure 13.6.

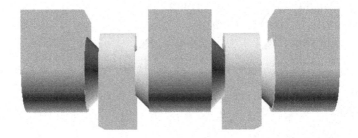

Figure 13.6

You still need to attach these to something, so let's just attach a block to each for demonstration purposes.

```
FullLink();
translate([0, 5, 0]) cube([20, CubeWidth, height]);
translate([4, -12, 0]) cube([12, CubeWidth, height]);
```

Note that the cube that gets attached to the pins portion is translated 5 mm on the Y-axis, and the cube that gets attached to the holes is translated –12 on the Y axis.

This gives you the model shown in Figure 13.7.

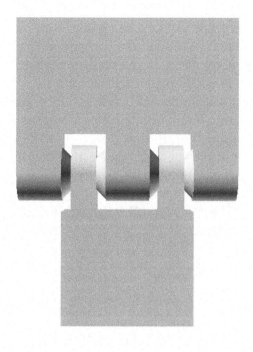

Figure 13.7

One point that can be important when you print is the precision of your 3D printer. This model has a very narrow gap between the pins and the holes and between the pin supports and the holes supports. Some printers or some printing materials may not be precise enough to create these gaps and may fuse the parts together. This is where the flexibility of the defined constants can come in. Observe that in Listing 13.1 I used defined constant for some parameters, like HoleSize and holeConnectorWidth. If you model does not have enough of a gap between the pins and the holes, you can increase the hole size a tenth of a mm or two or decrease the hole connector width by a tenth of a mm or two. If there is not enough of a gap between the supports, you can decrease the hole connector width by a small amount like a tenth of a mm or two.

You can also scale the entire link using the scale command. If you make it larger, you may be able to decrease the gaps slightly using these defined constants, since the scaling will increase the gap size too and it may be more than you need. If you make this hinge smaller, you will certainly need to increase these gaps.

The constant named height is the height of the hinge on the printer, which is actually the thickness of the hinge. Altering this can be very tricky, since it alters several parts. The same goes for holeConnectorLength. It is better to scale the whole thing than to try to tweak height or holeConnectorLength.

In the next chapter, I will use this hinge to make a simple toy robot.

Chapter 14

Robot

Now that we have hinges, let's make something with them. To keep it simple, we will make a little robot toy. Figure 14.1 shows what this looks like.

Figure 14.1

Here is the code in Listing 14.1.

```
HalfBodyWidth = 18;
ArmLength = 20;
LegLength = 35;
BodyLength = 45;

height = 5;
HoleSize = 3.4;
holeConnectorLength = 3.5;
holeConnectorWidth = 2.25;

module holeConnector(){
   difference(){
     union(){
       cube([holeConnectorWidth, holeConnectorLength,
       height]);
       translate([0,holeConnectorLength,height/2])
       rotate([0,90,0])
cylinder(h = holeConnectorWidth, d =height, $fn =
       99);
     } // End union
     translate([-1, holeConnectorLength, height/2])
     rotate([0, 90, 0])
     cylinder(h = holeConnectorWidth + 2, d = HoleSize,
     $fn = 50);
   }// End difference
} // End holesConnector module

module Holes(){
   translate([6 - holeConnectorWidth / 2,  -2.1,0])
   holeConnector();
   translate([14 – holeConnectorWidth / 2, -2.1, 0])
   holeConnector();
} // End Holes module

module cone(R,D){
   translate([D, 1.35, height / 2])
   rotate([0, R ,0])
   cylinder(h = 2.3, r1 = 2.3, r2 = 0, $fn = 99);
```

```
} // End cone module

module Pins(){
    $fn=99;
    translate([0,1.4,0])cube([4, 3.6, height]);
    translate([0,1.4,2.5]) rotate([0,90,0])
    cylinder(h = 4,d = 5);
    translate([8, 1.4, 0]) cube([4, 3.6, height]);
    translate([8, 1.4, 2.5]) rotate([0, 90, 0])
    cylinder(h = 4,d = 5);
    translate([16, 1.4, 0]) cube([4, 3.6, height]);
    translate([16, 1.4, 2.5]) rotate([0, 90, 0])
    cylinder(h = 4,d = 5);
    cone(90, 4);
    cone(-90, 8);
    cone(90, 12);
    cone(-90, 16.1);
} // End Pins module


module FullLink(){
    Holes();
    Pins();
} // End FullLink

module HalfRobot(){
    translate([0, -BodyLength, 0])
    cube([HalfBodyWidth, BodyLength, height]); //body
    translate([HalfBodyWidth+5,-20,0])
    rotate([0,0,90]) FullLink(); // Shoulder joint
    translate([HalfBodyWidth+7,-15,0])
    cube([ArmLength, 10, height]); //Arm
    difference(){ // Hand
        translate([HalfBodyWidth + ArmLength + 7, -17, 0])
        cube([10,15,height]);
        translate([HalfBodyWidth + ArmLength + 10,-12, -1])
        cube([10, 5, height + 2]);
    } // End hand
```

```
translate([HalfBodyWidth-20,-BodyLength-5,0])
FullLink(); //Leg joint
translate([HalfBodyWidth-15,-BodyLength-42,0])
cube([10,LegLength,height]); // Leg
translate([HalfBodyWidth - 15, -BodyLength –
LegLength - 7, 0])
cube([10, 5, 10]); // foot
cube([7, 15, height]); // Head
translate([4,10,0])
cylinder(h = height + 2, r=1, $fn = 99); // Eye
} // End half robot module
HalfRobot();
mirror([1,0,0]) HalfRobot();
```
Listing 14.1

The first four defined constants are parameters for the robot. HalfBodyWidth is half the width of the body. The reason it is half the width is that we actually build half the robot in this code, then mirror it to make the other half. This greatly reduces the amount of code you need and simplifies modifications. ArmLength is the length of the arms. LegLength is the length of the arms. BodyLength is the length (actually, the height when it is standing up) of the body. You can change any one of these and the rest of the body adapts. For example, if you change the arm length, the hands automatically more out to the new end of the arm. If you make the body wider, the entire arm assembly (joint, arm, and hand) moves out, as well as the legs. This is done by building these constants into the translate commands. This means that you can modify these four aspects of the robot just by changing these consents at the beginning of the code, and is an excellent example of the value of using these constants instead of just putting numbers in. In fact, one of the reasons for writing this chapter is to demonstrate the value of using constants, and also to demonstrate using the mirror command.

Everything from the height=5; line down to the line before module HalfRobot(){ is the code from the hinge from the previous chapter. If I remarked out the part of that file that actually called the module, I could have just used the include command discussed in Chapter 10 on duplicating objects. However, I wanted to have all the code visible in this listing.

After the code for the hinge, we come to the model HalfRobot. This module produces the part shown in Figure 14.2.

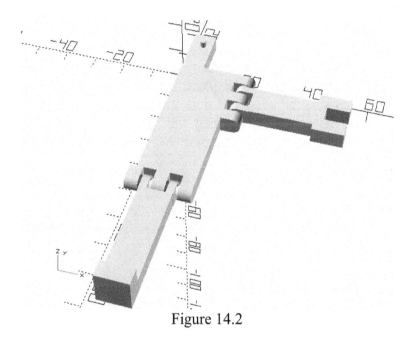

Figure 14.2

This module consists of simply putting together a lot of parts of the robot (mostly cubes) and then positioning the hinges to connect them. Note that I have remarked almost every line to make it easier to see what every part is.

The first cube is the main body, the torso (chest and hips). Then we have the shoulder joint, the hinge that connects the arm to the body. The hinge is simply rotated and translated to be in the right position. Notice that the translate command includes the HalfBodyWidth constant,

141

so if you change the body width the joint automatically moves. Then you have the arm, another simple cube. The arm is also translated by the half body width plus 7, the width of the hinge. Then you have the hand. This is made by having a cube and using the difference command to cut out a section, forming a little robot pincher. The hand is translated by the half body width plus the arm length plus the 7 mm for the hinge. Then you have the leg joint, another hinge. This is translated but does not need to be rotated since it is already in the proper orientation. Then you have the leg and at the end of the leg you have the foot. Finally, we add a cylinder to be the eye, a camera lens on the face.

Having defined the half robot module, we then just add the module command plus a mirror of the module for the other side. Notice that I built the half robot right on the Y-axis, so mirroring it along the X-axis fits the pieces together perfectly. We now have our first complete model of the book.

Chapter 15

Rotator

Now that we have hinges, let's move onto another moving part, the rotator. In this, shown in Figure 15.1, a shaft can rotate.

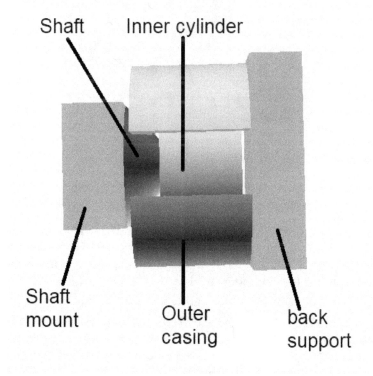

Figure 15.1

The inner cylinder rotates within the outer housing, allowing the shaft connected to the inner cylinder to rotate. You can attach anything to the shaft and to the backing of the outer casing. Let's look at the two individual components to get a clearer idea. Figure 15.2 shows the inner part, from below.

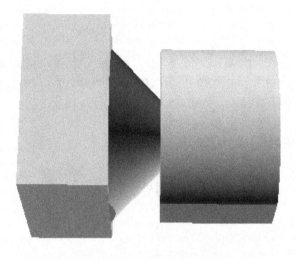

Figure 15.2

You can see that the shaft is cone shaped. As with the hinges, this to allow printing without having unsupported overhangs. The point of the gone extends far enough in the cylinder to have a large surface area of contact between the cone and the cylinder. Notice that the cylinder is slightly flattened on the bottom. This again is to allow proper printing. If the cylinder were completely round on the bottom, it could move or roll as it was being printed. Slightly flattening the bottom allows for some surface to adhere and holds it stead enough to print. The cone is also slightly flattened because it has to be connected to the center of the cylinder, so it has to be on the same level. For this example, a simple cube is attached to hold the cylinder up as it is printed. In you application, anything can be attached. Figure 15.3 shows the outer casing.

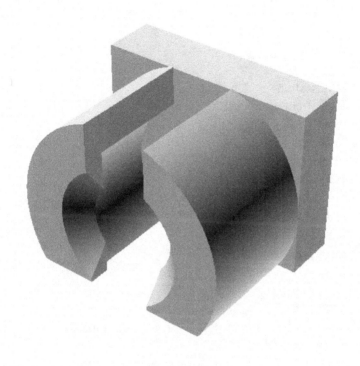

Figure 15.3

From this angle, you can clearly see the cut out section inside where the cylinder goes. You can see the front wall has a cut out section that matches the cone-shaped shaft. The bottom is flat for the same reason as the cylinder, to keep it from rolling during printing. The slit in the bottom is to allow the cylinder to rest on the print bed. The slit in the top is to reduce unsupported overhang that could sag during printing. Often a small circular hole shape can be printed and the overhang is so short it does not sag. For this model, however, we want to be able to make it as large as we like, so I have eliminated most of the horizontal section of the cylinder. Now let's look at the code.

```
$fn = 999;
Size = 2;
CasingRadius = 5 * Size;
slot = 3 * Size;
EndGap = .8;
RadiusGap = .8;
RotatorRadius = 3 * Size;
RotatorLength = 4 * Size;
ShaftRadius = RotatorRadius * 1.5;
ShaftLength = ShaftRadius * .7;
sink = .2 * Size;
ShaftSupportWidth = 10;

module Casing(){
   difference(){
      translate([-ShaftLength/2,0,RotatorRadius])
      rotate([0,90,0])
      cylinder(h = RotatorLength + ShaftLength / 2 +
      EndGap, r = CasingRadius);


      translate([-EndGap,0,RotatorRadius])
      rotate([0,90,0])
      cylinder(h = RotatorLength + ShaftLength + EndGap,
      r = RotatorRadius + RadiusGap); //Rotator cutout

      translate([-ShaftLength,0,RotatorRadius])
      rotate([0,90,0]) cylinder(h = ShaftRadius +
      RadiusGap, r1 = ShaftRadius + RadiusGap, r2 = 0);
      //  Shaft cutout

      translate([-ShaftLength,-slot/2,-CasingRadius/2])
      cube([RotatorLength + ShaftLength * 2 + EndGap,
      slot, CasingRadius*3]); //Slot
```

```
    } // End difference
  }  // End casing module

module InnerRotator(){
    translate([0,0,RotatorRadius]) rotate([0,90,0])
    cylinder(h = RotatorLength, r = RotatorRadius);

    translate([-ShaftLength,0,RotatorRadius])
    rotate([0,90,0])
    cylinder(h = ShaftRadius,r1=ShaftRadius,r2=0);
} // End Rotator inner module

module Rotator(){
    difference(){
        translate([0,0,-sink])
        union(){
            Casing();
            InnerRotator();
        } // End union
        translate([-50,-50,-100])cube(100);
    } // End difference
} // End Rotator

Rotator();
translate([-ShaftLength-ShaftSupportWidth,
-ShaftRadius,0])
cube([ShaftSupportWidth, ShaftRadius * 2,ShaftRadius * 2
– sink * 2]); //Shaft support
translate([RotatorLength + EndGap, -CasingRadius, 0])
cube([CasingRadius / 2, CasingRadius * 2, CasingRadius *
1.5]); // Casing support
```
Listing 15.1

First, you see we have a lot of defined constants. Many of these you can change to modify your rotator. The constant $fn is, as explained in chapter 2, defines the resolution of cylinders, spheres, and a few other shapes. We want the cylinders in this model to be very smooth, so we want this to be very large. Unless you are having serious problems with rendering times, I do not advise changing this. Size is a multiplier that scales up the entire model. It changes everything except the gap between parts, as I will explain shortly. You can use this to make the rotator bigger or smaller while maintaining proportion. CasingRadius is the outside radius of the casing. You can change this if you like to make a bigger casing if you want a stronger casing. It does not affect the performance of the rotator. The constant slot is the width of the slot at the top of the casing. The value I have selected works pretty well, but you can experiment with it if you like. A narrower slot is a little better if you printer can manage the overhang.

EndGap is the distance between the inner cylinder and the inner walls of the casing at each end of the cylinder. RadiusGap is the distance between the outer radius of the inner rotator cylinder and the casing walls around the circumference of the rotator cylinder. Note that these are the only constants that are not multiplied by Size. It does not matter how big your model gets using the Size constant, the gap can remain the same. How big a gap you need depends on the quality of your printer and the settings you use in your slicer. If you have a very high-resolution printer and set values like layer size very small in your slicer, you will have a very precise model and can get away with a smaller gap. Having a smaller gap will give you a better rotator, with less wiggle in the shaft. This is something you can experiment with by printing simple rotators with different gap sizes to se how small a gap you can get away with and not have the parts fuse together.

RotatorRadius is the radius of the inside rotator cylinder. You can play with this size, but be careful. Obviously, the inner rotator cannot be larger than the outer wall of the casing. In fact, if you make it too close to the size of the outer casing, you will have very thin and fragile walls. RotatorLength is the length of the inner rotator cylinder. If you change the length of this, the outer casing automatically adjusts to be just a little longer, so this is one of the easier constants to play with. A longer rotator cylinder can be more stable, with less wiggle in the shaft. You can experiment with this, adjusting the rotator length to see how it affects the rotator performance.

ShaftRadius is the radius of the bottom of the cone that forms the shaft. In order for the cone to go up at a 45-degree angle for stable printing, the height of the cone is automatically set to the same value as the radius of the base of the cone. ShaftLength is the distance from the base of the cone to the point where it enters the rotator cylinder. Notice that it is automatically adjusted to fit the radius of the shaft by multiplying the shaft radius by a fraction value. If this value were 1, the point of the cone would just be touching the rotator cylinder and would not really be connected to it. The lower the value of this fraction, the shorter the shaft is but the larger the area is where the shaft connects to the rotator cylinder and therefore the stronger the connection of the cone to the rotator cylinder is at this point. You can fiddle with this, and the rest of the model will adjust. However, there are some limits. As you make the shaft shorter, the wall of the outer casing that the shaft goes through get thinner and the hole the shaft goes through gets larger. If the fraction value is below about .55, the hole in the casing is larger than the rotator cylinder and this cylinder can simply slide out of the casing. I recommend a value no smaller than .7.

The constant sink is the amount of bottom that is cut off of the inner rotator cylinder to flatten the cylinder and keep it steady during printing. In is the amount the model sinks below the XY-axis in order to be cut off, as will be explained shortly. You can experiment with this a little if you like, but I think I have hit a pretty good sweet spot on this where you get a steady print without significantly affecting the rotation of the inner cylinder.

ShaftSupportWidth is the width of the cube supporting the shaft code at the base. The reason I have used a constant for this is that the support must be translated by a distance that depends on how wide it is. By having this defined constant, you can change the thickness of this support and automatically have it moved to the correct location. The value of 10 in this example is arbitrary, and you will change it to suit whatever you attach the rotator shaft to.

This model is ideal to use modules, since it has several detached parts. The first module is the outer casing without the back support. The second module is the inner rotator without the back support. The third module is where you put them together and cut off a little of the bottom to make the flat bottom for printing. The third module still does not have the supports, because the size and shapes of the supports depends on what you want to attach the rotator to.

The casing module uses the difference command to first make a cylinder of radius CasingRadius and a length equal to the rotator length plus half the shaft length plus the length of the end gap. This is the outer casing. Having the length set by this equation causes the casing to automatically adjust when you change any of these parameters. It then subtracts from this the cylinder cutout, then the shaft cutout, then the slot cutout. Notice that in most cases, the size of the cutout is the size of the part that will go in that space plus the gap size. The result of this module is what you saw in Figure 15.3.

The InnerRotator module simply combines the rotator cylinder with the shaft cone. This is what you see in Figure 15.2.

The Rotator module combines the other two modules into a union, lowers this union by the amount sink so that this amount is below the XY plane, and then uses the difference command to remove everything below the XY plane. The result is shown in Figure 15.4.

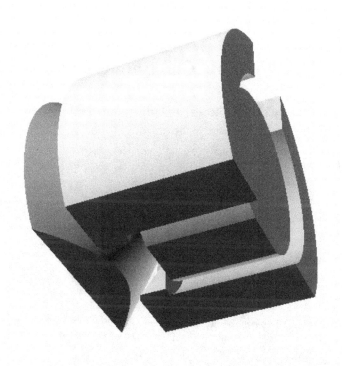

Figure 15.4

Notice that this is missing the support for both the shaft and the casing. This is done to give you versatility. You can use the Rotator module in any of your projects by attaching whatever you like to the two ends. Be sure that whatever you attach to the end of the casing connects the two sides of the casing, which are not connected in this module. Otherwise, they will simply fall apart and the rotator cylinder will fall out. In the next chapter, I will use this rotator to construct a practical device, a cell phone adjustable stand.

Chapter 16

Adjustable Cell Phone Stand

Figure 16.1 shows an adjustable cell phone stand that employs four of the rotators developed in the previous chapters.

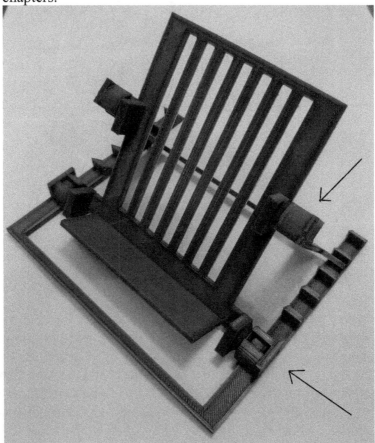

Figure 16.1

There are two rotators on each side, one on the base and one on the side. The notched base allows you to select where you put the support, and therefore what angle the cell phone sits at. This is not a particularly complex project. The hardest part is positioning the rotators right. Figure 16.2 shows the holder in the position it is in when it is printed.

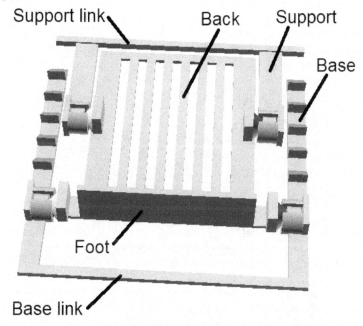

Figure 16.2

Listing 16.1 shows the code for this.

```
$fn = 999;
Size = 1.75;
HolderRadius = 5 * Size;
CasingRadius = 5 * Size;
slot = 3 * Size;
EndGap = .8;
RadiusGap = 1;
RotatorRadius = 3 * Size;
RotatorLength = 4 * Size;
ShaftRadius = RotatorRadius * 1.5;
```

153

```
ShaftLength = ShaftRadius * .7;
ShaftSupportWidth = 5;
sink = .2 * Size;
PhoneWidth = 78;
Width = PhoneWidth + 12;
BackHeight = 110;
BackThickness = 2;
FootHeight = 25 + BackThickness;
BaseWidth = 10;
BaseLength = 83;
SupportLength = 50;
RotatorX  = - Width / 2 - 6;
BaseX = -Width / 2 - 14;

module Casing(){
  difference(){
    translate([-ShaftLength / 2, 0, RotatorRadius])
    rotate([0, 90, 0])
    cylinder(h = RotatorLength + ShaftLength / 2 +
    EndGap,
    r = CasingRadius);

    translate([-EndGap, 0, RotatorRadius]) rotate([0,90,0])
    cylinder(h = RotatorLength + ShaftLength + EndGap,
    r = RotatorRadius + RadiusGap); //Rotator cutout

    translate([-ShaftLength,0,RotatorRadius])
    rotate([0,90,0])
    cylinder(h = ShaftRadius + RadiusGap,
    r1 = ShaftRadius + RadiusGap, r2 = 0); // Shaft cutout

    translate([-ShaftLength, -slot / 2, -CasingRadius / 2])
    cube([RotatorLength + ShaftLength * 2 + EndGap,
    slot, CasingRadius * 3]); //Slot

  } // End difference
} // End casing module
```

```
module InnerRotator(){
  translate([0,0,RotatorRadius])
  rotate([0,90,0])
  cylinder(h=RotatorLength,r=RotatorRadius);

  translate([-ShaftLength, 0, RotatorRadius])
  rotate([0,90,0])
  cylinder(h=ShaftRadius,r1=ShaftRadius,r2=0);
} // End Rotator inner module

module Rotator(){
  difference(){
    translate([0,0,-sink])
    union(){
      Casing();
      InnerRotator();
    } // End union
    translate([-50, -50, -100]) cube(100);
  } // End difference
} // End Rotator
module FullRotator(){
  rotate([0,0,180]){
    Rotator();
    translate([-ShaftLength - ShaftSupportWidth,
    -ShaftRadius, 0])
    cube([ShaftSupportWidth, ShaftRadius * 2,
    ShaftRadius * 2 – sink * 2]); //Shaft support
    translate([RotatorLength + EndGap,-CasingRadius,0])
    cube([3,CasingRadius*2,CasingRadius*1.5]);
  }
} // End FullRotator

module Base(){
  difference(){
    translate([RotatorX-11,4.5,0])FullRotator();
    translate([RotatorX-6,-8,-8.5]) rotate([35,0,0])
    cube([6,10,10]);
  } // End difference
```

```
    translate([BaseX + 3,0,0])
    cube([15, 12, BackThickness]);

    translate([BaseX-14,11,0])
    cube([BaseWidth,BaseLength,3]);

    translate([BaseX-14,-FootHeight-2,0])
    cube([BaseWidth,FootHeight,3]);

    for(Y = [27 : 1.5 * BaseWidth : BaseLength + 4]){
    // Notch wedges
      difference(){
        translate([BaseX-14,Y,0])cube(BaseWidth);
        translate([BaseX-15,Y+BaseWidth,0])
        rotate([45,0,0])
        cube([BaseWidth+4,BaseWidth,2*BaseWidth]);
      } //End difference
    } // End for
} // End Base module

module Support(){
    translate([RotatorX + 1.8, BackHeight -SupportLength,
0])
    FullRotator();

    translate([-Width/2 - 15, BackHeight –SupportLength +
    6,0])
    cube([13, SupportLength, 3]);
} // End support module

difference(){// Back
    translate([-Width / 2, 0, 0])
    cube([Width,BackHeight, BackThickness]);
    for (X=[-30 : 10 : 30]){
      translate([X, BackHeight / 2 + 5, 0])
      cube([5, BackHeight - 20, BackThickness * 2 + 2],
      center = true); // slats
    } // End for
```

```
} // End difference

translate([-Width / 2, 0, 0]) cube([Width, 3, FootHeight]);
//Foot

Base();
mirror([1, 0 ,0]) Base();
translate([-Width / 2 - 28, - FootHeight -7,0])
cube([Width + 56, 5, 3]); //Base brace
Support();
mirror([1, 0, 0]) Support();
translate([-Width / 2 - 27, BackHeight + 4, 0])
cube([Width - (BaseX + 4), 4, 4]); //Support link
```
Listing 16.1

You can see that the first 13 lines are the constants for the rotators. I will not go into these again here, since they were discussed in the previous chapter. I have adjusted few of them, like size and RadiusGap, to fit this model. As explained in the previous chapter, some of these were intended to be adjusted for individual projects.

The ten lines after these are constants that define the shape and size of the phone holder. The most important of these, and the one you are most likely to want to change, is PhoneWidth. This is the width of your phone that you want to sit on the holder. Measure the width of your phone and insert that number there, perhaps adding a mm or two to make sure it fits. The only time this is used in the code is the next line that calculates Width, the total width of the back of the holder. The reason the total width is more than the phone width is that the rotators extend 6 mm into the backing to anchor them, and the phone must fit between these. Actually, it does not absolutely have to fit between these, but if it does not, it will be tilted forward in front of them. You can actually do this if you want to sit your phone sideways, it is just not as secure.

BackHeight is the height of the back of the phone holder. I do not recommend adjusting this, because it messes with how the support fits into the base. If you made it taller, the phone cannot lean as far forward. BackThickness controls how thick the back of the holder where the phone leans against is. Making this thicker will make the holder stronger, but I have found that 2 mm has always been enough. However, you can increase this slightly if you like. FootHeight is the height of the foot where the bottom of the phone sits. You can make this higher if you have a very thick phone. BaseWidth is the width of the bases. Increasing this slightly could make the bases a little stronger, but more than another 2 mm would case the base to merge with the support. BaseLength is the length of the bases. You can increase this to as much as 98, which would add another tab, but using that has the phone practically lying down. Increasing it beyond about 100 could merge it with the cross bar. The current value is usually satisfactory. SupportLength is the length of the supports. Changing that can change the way the support fits into the base, and is not recommended. RotatorX is the X-axis translation of two of the rotators, and BaseX is the X translation of the bases. As you can see, these are computed from the width, and you should not change these.

This discussion of constants that you can change and ones that you should not is a good time to go over the reasons for using constants. One reason is that you actually want to be able to change something in your model easily to make various versions, like the PhoneWidth constant. Another is to allow you to make adjustments in your model to get it right, but that you will not want to fiddle with once you have found a good value. An example of that here is SupportLength. There are often cases, like this, where the value of the constant affects several things. The constant SupportLength is used three times in the code because changing the length of the support requires repositioning or changing other things. If I did not use the constant, I would have to go through the code and change each of these each time I changed the length of the support trying to get it just right. Defining a constant and using it everywhere that the

158

value must change in the same way both saves time and reduces the chance of making a mistake in the code. The third reason is simply to document your code. Having descriptive constant names makes it much easier to go back later and see what the various parameters mean.

After the constants, the next four modules are the rotator modules, straight out of last chapter. I made a few minor changes. In the full rotator module, I rotated the rotator 180 degrees to turn it around to face the way I needed it for this project. The shaft and casing supports are also adjusted to make them the right size for this project.

After the rotator modules are two modules for this specific project, the base and the support. Since there are two of each of these, it makes sense to make them modules and reuse them.

The first thing in the Base is the rotator attached to it. The reason for the difference command applied to the rotator is to cut off a tiny bit of the corner that gets in the way when you rotate the back to an upright position. After the rotator are a series of cubes that form the base. Finally, a for loop is used to add the series of triangular notches to the base so you can fit the support into any one of these to set the right angle. The notches are formed by making a cube and then cutting out part of it with another cube using the difference command. The Support module simply consists of adding a rotator to a long, flat cube.

After these modules, the back is formed by making a large, flat cube and using the difference command to cut out a lot of rectangular holes. The for loop is used to add these holes, rather than defining each one individually. These holes are not actually necessary and can be eliminated, but they allow for air flow to cool your phone and cut down on the amount of material required to make the holder. After the back, next line adds the foot. Then a base and a mirrored brace are added. The next line is the base link, which holds the two bases firmly in position. Next a support and mirrored support are added.

Finally, the support link is added. This is a very important part. It not only holds the supports on position, the ends extend out beyond the supports. This is what fits into the notches and holds the back up to angle your phone.

Chapter 17

Ball Joint

In chapter 15, I explained how to make a rotator that can rotate 360 degrees in one plane. In this chapter, I will explain how to make a ball joint that can move in all three dimensions. Figure 17.1 shows the basic design.

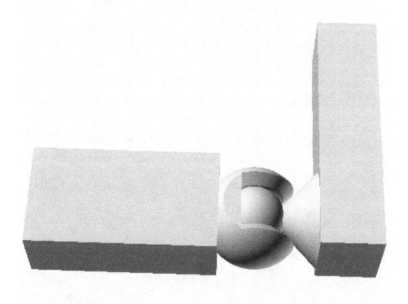

Figure 17.1

In this model, I have two rectangular boxes attached at a right angle. One is attached to the rotator shaft, the other to the rotator casing, much like the rotator in chapter 15. Of course, you could attach anything you want to these, but these boxes make for an easy demonstration.

Figures 17.2 and 17.2 show the top box rotated much like the previous rotator, perpendicular to the other box.

Figure 17.2

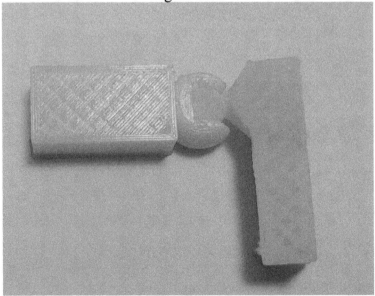

Figure 17.3

Figure 17.4 shows the boxes at an angle. Figure 17.5 shows the boxes turned so they are pointing in opposite directions.

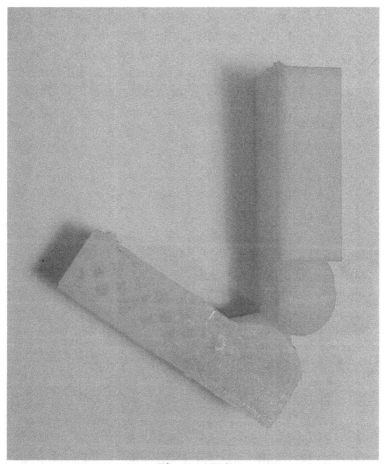

Figure 17.4

Figure 17.5

In Figure 17.5 you can see that the second box is rotating in a plane perpendicular to the plane it was rotating in Figure 17.2 and 17.3. In short, you can rotate the second part of your model in all sorts of directions with this ball joint. Listing 17.1 gives the total code for this ball joint.

```
$fn = 99;
CasingRadius = 8;
BallRadius = 5;
Extrude = .5;
gap = .8;
sink = .6;

ShaftRadius = BallRadius * 1.5;
ShiftCut = BallRadius * .3;
CasingSupportLength = 30;

module BallCasing(){
   difference(){
   intersection(){
     sphere(CasingRadius);
     union(){
        translate([-4. 45 * BallRadius, -2 * BallRadius,
        -BallRadius + sink])
        cube([BallRadius * 4, BallRadius * 4, CasingRadius
        * 1.4]);

        translate([0,-ShiftCut,0])
        rotate([-90,0,0])
        cylinder(h = CasingRadius + ShiftCut, r1 = 0, r2 =
        CasingRadius + ShiftCut);
        translate([0,ShiftCut,0]) rotate([90,0,0])
        cylinder(h = CasingRadius + ShiftCut, r1 = 0, r2 =
        CasingRadius + ShiftCut);
     } // End union
   } // End intersection

   sphere(BallRadius+gap);
```

```
      } //End difference
   } // End BallCasing module

module Ball(){
   sphere(BallRadius);
   translate([Extrude * BallRadius, 0, 0]) rotate([0, 90, 0])
   cylinder(h = ShaftRadius, r1 = 0, r2 = ShaftRadius);
} // End Ball module

module BallJoint(){
   difference(){
      translate([0,0,BallRadius-sink]){
         BallCasing();
         Ball();
      } // End translate
      translate([-CasingRadius, -CasingRadius,
      -CasingRadius * 2])

      cube([ShaftRadius + CasingRadius * 2, CasingRadius
      * 2, CasingRadius * 2]);
   } // End difference
} // End BallJoint module

BallJoint();

translate([Extrude * BallRadius + ShaftRadius,
-ShaftRadius, 0])
cube([10, ShaftRadius * 6, 1.7 * ShaftRadius - sink]);
//Shaft support

translate([-CasingSupportLength-BallRadius - gap,
-CasingRadius, 0])
cube([CasingSupportLength, 2 * CasingRadius, 1.4 *
CasingRadius - sink]); //Casing Support
```
Listing 17.1

Much like the rotator, this has three modules. BallCasing is for the outer casing, Ball is for the inner ball and the cone-shaped shaft that connects to it. Then BallJoint puts the two together, sinks them a little, and cuts off the bottom to give the ball a slight flattening on the bottom to hold it steady during printing.

There are nine constants, some of which you can adjust and some of which are automatically computed. You may recall that $fn is the number of segments in a sphere, cylinder, or cone. In previous examples, this was set to 999. In this one, I set it to 99. The reason is that the more segments you have, the slower the rendering. This project has so many cones and spheres that a larger number of segments results in an absurdly long rendering time. CasingRadius is the radius of the outer casing. BallRadius is the radius of the inner ball that rotates within the casing. Extrude is how far the shaft cone is pulled out of the inner ball. If this were 0, the tip of the cone would be at the center of the ball. If this were 1, the tip of the shaft cone would be just touching the outside of the ball. The lower the value of Extrude, the wider the surface connection of the shaft is to the ball, making a stronger connection, but the short the shaft. I found .5 to be a good value, but you can play around with it. The constant gap is the distance between the outside of the inner ball and the inside of the hollowed-out casing. A lower value makes for a tighter fit, but increases the chances of the ball and the casing becoming fused together during printing. Factors such as your slicer setting (like layer height), your nozzle size, your temperature, your material, and so on will determine how small you can make gap. As explained, sink determines how much of the bottom is sliced off to make the ball flat enough to not roll away during printing. The lower the value of sink, the rounder your ball will be. This can make for a smoother rotation, but it increases the chances of a print failure. Factors like bed adhesion can determine how low sink can go and still work for you. ShaftRadius is the radius of the wider end of the shaft cone. The height of this cone is directly proportional to this value, so increasing this value increases the length of the shaft. You can play around with this to see the effects and see what suits your project. CasingSupportLength is the length of the cube attached to the casing. This depends on what you are building, and therefore what length or width you want it to be. The reason that this is a constant defied at the beginning is that the component attached to the casing MUST be moved to a very specific location that depends on the length of this piece, as well as some other variables like the gap. In order to make sure that it is positioned properly, I have Created equations in the code that automatically position it, and created this constant for you to set at the beginning. ShiftCut determines the positions of some of the pieces inside the structure. I will explain it later when I describe those pieces. However, this is a value that you should not mess with.

Now let's get into the code. The Ball module simply creates a sphere with a cone stuck in it, shown in Figure 17.6. This is basically the same as the rotator in chapter 15, but with a ball instead of a cylinder.

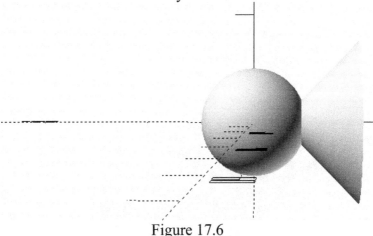

Figure 17.6

The BallCasing is quite complex, and uses most of the shaping techniques discussed in the earlier chapters such as union, intersection, and difference, which makes it a good educational example. These are layered like the

167

layers of an onion, and it is best to start with the inner layer and work our way out to explain it.

First, you have the union in the code

```
union(){
    translate([-4.45 * BallRadius, -2 * BallRadius, -1 *
    BallRadius])
    cube([BallRadius * 4, BallRadius * 4, CasingRadius *
    1.4]);

    translate([0, -ShiftCut, 0]) rotate([-90, 0, 0])
    cylinder(h = CasingRadius + ShiftCut, r1 = 0, r2 =
    CasingRadius + ShiftCut);

    translate([0, ShiftCut, 0]) rotate([90, 0, 0])
    cylinder(h = CasingRadius + ShiftCut, r1 = 0, r2 =
    CasingRadius + ShiftCut);
} // End union
```
Listing 17.2

This code gives you the odd-looking shape in Figure 17.7.

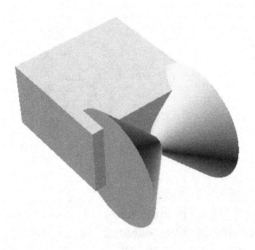

Figure 17.7

Here I created two cones that are upside-down in that the bottom is zero radius and the top is larger. I rotate one 90 degrees one way and the other 90 degrees the other. This would have the tips of the two cones meeting at the origin (X, Y, and Z equal 0). However, I translate them together by moving each one by ShiftCut toward the origin. I also add a cube. I then use the intersection command to eliminate anything outside a sphere of radius CasingRadius. This results in the shape shown in Figure 17.8.

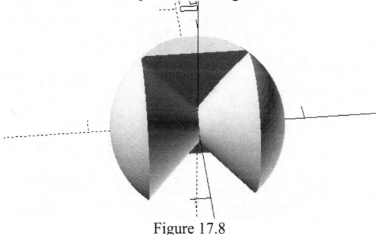

Figure 17.8

Then I use difference to remove a sphere of radius BallRadius + gap, which gives me the shape in Figure 17.9.

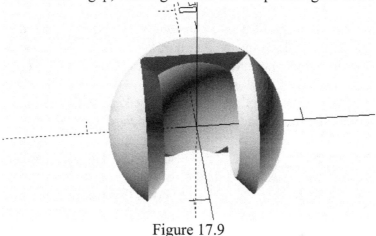

Figure 17.9

The reason for all this complex use of union, intersection, and difference was to get a slot for the shaft that expands outward from the center to fit the shaft, which also expands as it goes away from the ball. Figure 17.10 shows the two pieces fitting together.

Figure 17.10

You might notice that this structure is centered on the Z axis, which means that half the structure is below the Z axis. We cannot have that. In addition, we need to flatten the bottom of the spheres so they do not roll during printing. The module BallJoint takes the two parts, combines them, and shifts them upward by BallRadius – sink. That means that the center rotating ball is just sink below the X-Y plane. This also means that the shaft and casing are also cut off at the same level. BallJoint is now our finished part. Figure 17.11 shows this from the bottom.

Figure 17.11

Now all you need to do is attach something to the shaft and casing. You are very flexible in this. The only requirement is that the object attached to the shaft must be translated Extrude*BallRadius+ShaftRadius in the X direction from the center of the ball and the object attached to the casing must be translated BallRadius + gap + the width of the object in the negative X direction from the center of the ball. Note that the X coordinate of the center of the ball is 0 until you move the ball joint.

I did not include a Size constant in this model the way I did with the rotator, but you can always simply scale the entire model. You can then divide gap by the scale factor to keep the gap small.

As shown in Figure 17.2 through Figure 17.5, this ball joint can rotate360 degrees around one axis, and can shift about 90 degrees either way and rotate around another axis, However, it still cannot rotate in every direction because it cannot be tilted upward as seen in Figure 17.1.

171

However, suppose the casing itself could be rotated? Then you could actually rotate the shaft in any direction at all. This could be accomplished by connecting the ball joint to the rotator from chapter 15. This is shown in Figure 17.12.

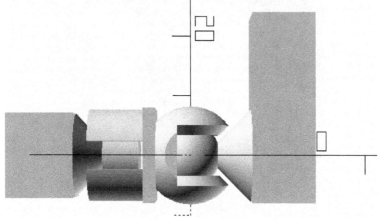

Figure 17.12

The code for this is shown in Listing 17.3.

```
$fn = 99;

BallCasingRadius = 8;
BallRadius = 5;
Extrude = .5;
gap = .8;
BallSink = .6;

BallShaftRadius = BallRadius * 1.5;
ShiftCut = BallRadius * .3;
CasingSupportLength = 2;

Size = 1.5;
CasingRadius = 5 * Size;
slot = 3 * Size;
EndGap = .8;
RadiusGap = .8;
RotatorRadius = 3 * Size;
```

```
RotatorLength = 4 * Size;
ShaftRadius = RotatorRadius * 1.5;
ShaftLength = ShaftRadius * .7;
sink = .2 * Size;
ShaftSupportWidth = 15;

module Casing(){
   difference(){
      translate([-ShaftLength / 2, 0, RotatorRadius])
      rotate([0,90,0])
      cylinder(h = RotatorLength + ShaftLength / 2 +
      EndGap, r = CasingRadius);

      translate([-EndGap, 0, RotatorRadius])
      rotate([0,90,0])
      cylinder(h = RotatorLength + ShaftLength + EndGap,
      r = RotatorRadius + RadiusGap); //Rotator cutout

      translate([-ShaftLength, 0, RotatorRadius])
      rotate([0,90,0])
      cylinder(h = ShaftRadius + RadiusGap, r1 =
      ShaftRadius + RadiusGap, r2 = 0); // Shaft cutout

      translate([-ShaftLength, -slot / 2, -CasingRadius / 2])
      cube([RotatorLength + ShaftLength * 2 + EndGap, slot,
      CasingRadius * 3]); //Slot

   } // End difference
}  // End casing module

module InnerRotator(){
   translate([0, 0, RotatorRadius]) rotate([0, 90, 0])
   cylinder(h = RotatorLength, r = RotatorRadius);

   translate([-ShaftLength,0,RotatorRadius])
   rotate([0,90,0]) cylinder(h = ShaftRadius, r1 =
   ShaftRadius, r2 = 0);
} // End Rotator inner module
```

```
module Rotator(){
  difference(){
    translate([0,0,-sink])
    union(){
      Casing();
      InnerRotator();
    } // End union
    translate([-50, -50, -100]) cube(100);
  } // End difference
} // End Rotator

module BallCasing(){
  difference(){
    intersection(){
      sphere(BallCasingRadius);
      union(){
        translate([-4.45 * BallRadius, -2 * BallRadius,
        -BallRadius + BallSink])
        cube([BallRadius * 4, BallRadius * 4,
        BallCasingRadius * 1.4]);

        translate([0, -ShiftCut, 0]) rotate([-90 ,0, 0])
        cylinder(h = BallCasingRadius + ShiftCut, r1 = 0,
        r2 = BallCasingRadius + ShiftCut);

        translate([0,ShiftCut,0])rotate([90,0,0])
        cylinder(h = BallCasingRadius + ShiftCut, r1 = 0,
        r2 = BallCasingRadius + ShiftCut);
      } // End union
    } // End intersection

    sphere(BallRadius+gap);
  } //End difference
} // End BallCasing module

module Ball(){
  sphere(BallRadius);
```

```
    translate([Extrude * BallRadius, 0, 0])
    rotate([0, 90, 0])
    cylinder(h = BallShaftRadius, r1 = 0, r2 =
    BallShaftRadius);
} // End Ball module

module BallJoint(){
    difference(){
        translate([0,0,BallRadius-BallSink]){
            BallCasing();
            Ball();
        } // End translate
        translate([-BallCasingRadius,-BallCasingRadius,
        -BallCasingRadius*2])
        cube([BallShaftRadius + BallCasingRadius * 2,
        BallCasingRadius * 2, BallCasingRadius * 2]);
    } // End difference
} // End BallJoint module


BallJoint();

translate([-CasingSupportLength – BallRadius – gap –
RotatorLength - EndGap, 0, 0]) Rotator();

translate([-ShaftLength – ShaftSupportWidth –
CasingSupportLength – BallRadius – gap – RotatorLength
- EndGap, -ShaftRadius,0])
cube([ShaftSupportWidth, ShaftRadius * 2, ShaftRadius *
2 – sink * 2 - 2]); //Shaft support

translate([Extrude * BallRadius + BallShaftRadius,
-BallShaftRadius, 0])
cube([10, BallShaftRadius * 4, 1.7 * BallShaftRadius -
BallSink]); //Shaft support

translate([-CasingSupportLength – BallRadius - gap, -
CasingRadius, 0])
```

```
cube([CasingSupportLength, 2 * CasingRadius,
CasingRadius * 1.5]); //Casing Support
```
Listing 17.3

This is done by combining the code in Listing 17.1 with the code in Listing 15.1. Of course, it is not quite that simple. For one thing, the code used some of the same defined constant and module names. This would have created major clashes. To avoid that, I renamed a few things by adding a little descriptive adjective to some of the names in Listing 17.1 to make them different, like changing ShaftRadius to BallShaftRadius and the module Casing to BallCasing. I also deleted the $fn=999; line so the only setting of $fn was 99. Of course, it was necessary to reposition the rotator unit to have it fit on the end of the ball joint unit. It is also necessary to remove the casing support from the ball joint, since the rotator holder is attached to the casing of the ball joint. To change the size of this model, simply scale the entire model. To change the relative sizes of the rotator and ball joint parts (which is very unlikely to be useful), change the Size constant to change the size of the rotator part. Since this is really just a combination of the code from chapters 15 and 17, I will not go into any more detail.

Chapter 18

Wheel and Fidget Spinner

In this chapter, I would like to introduce yet another type of rotator. I know this might seem a bit redundant after the rotator and ball joint, but both of those had a flat portion of the rotating component. This one does not, and is printed in a different orientation, which can come in handy sometimes. While the other rotator was printed lying on its side, this one is flat on the print bed. This allows you to print objects that have parts extruding from the edge of the wheel. An example I will use in this chapter is a fidget spinner. I will refer to the main part that I will be describing as the wheel. Figure 18.1 shows the wheel and axle.

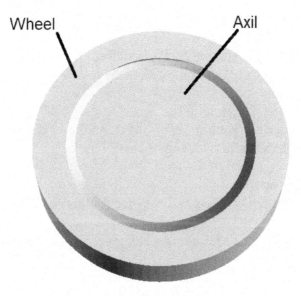

Figure 18.1

Figure 18.2 shows a cross section of the wheel and axle. Observe that the axle is wider in the middle, as is the hole in the wheel. This holds the axle in place.

Figure 18.2

The code for this is fairly simple, and is shown in Listing 18.1.

```
AxleRadius=10;
Height=5;
WheelRadius=15;
Gap=1.1;
$fn=99;

module Wheel(){
   cylinder(h = Height/2, r1 = AxleRadius, r2 = AxleRadius
   + Height / 2);// Bottom of shaft

   translate([0,0,Height/2])
   cylinder(h = Height / 2, r1 = AxleRadius + Height / 2,
   r2 = AxleRadius); // Top of shaft

   difference(){
      cylinder(h = Height, r = WheelRadius); // Wheel
      cylinder(h = Height / 2 + .001, r1 = AxleRadius +
      Gap, r2 = AxleRadius + Height /2 + Gap); // Bottom
      of cutout

      translate([0, 0, Height / 2])
```

```
cylinder(h = Height / 2, r1 = AxleRadius + Height/2 +
Gap, r2 = AxleRadius + Gap); // Top of cutout

translate([0, 0, -1])
cylinder(h = Height + 2, r = AxleRadius + Gap);
//Extend cutout

    } // End difference
} // End Wheel module
```
Listing 18.1

First, we have some defined constants that make it easy to change the wheel, as well as making the code more readable. First we have AxleRadius, which is obviously the radius of the axle. Height is the height of the wheel as it is lying on its side. WheelRadius is the outer radius of the wheel. Gap is the gap between the axle and the inner hole on the wheel that the axle fits into. Then you have the usual $fn that determines how many segments the cylinders have, and therefore how smooth they are.

Naturally, we put the wheel component into a module so you can use it easily. The axle is coded first. The first line is the bottom of the axle and the second is the top. We use cylinders with different radii at the top and bottom to cause the axle to be wider in the middle.

After the axle, we have the outer wheel, which is more complicated. We use the difference command to create the wheel and then cut out the shaped hole for the axle. The first line within the difference command is the simple cylinder that everything will be cut out of. Then you have the bottom of the hole for the axle, which is the same shape as the axle but larger by the amount Gap. You might notice that the height of this has a tiny bit (.001 mm) added to it. This is to ensure overlap with the top to avoid the problem discussed earlier where whether something is cut out is clearly defined. Next we have the part of the hole that fits the top of the axle. Then we have one more cylinder that extends 1 mm below and 1 mm above the wheel, again to ensure that there is no ambiguity about the fact that you are cutting out a hole that goes all the way through the wheel.

I would like to go into the Gap a little bit, because setting it can be difficult. You want this to be as small as possible and not have the parts fuse together during printing. As with the other models, how small you can make this depends on the quality of your printer and the settings you give your slicer, such as layer height. I often find with this wheel that the axle will be fused to the wheel in places so that the wheel does not turn at first. However, if I turn the axle very hard, these places break off and the wheel turns freely after that. Still, you may need to increase the gap if it is sticking too hard. The more you increase it, the looser the axle will be. The gap absolutely must be smaller than ¼ of the height of the wheel, or it will literally fall out. Therefore, increasing the height will allow for a greater gap. Also, the larger the axle is, the less the axle can tilt, so making the axle as large as you can helps. However, the outer radius of the wheel must be larger than the radius of the axle plus ¼ of the height, or the top and bottom of the wheel will not be connected. In practice, the wheel should be several mm larger than the radius of the axle plus ¼ of the height.

Now that we have the wheel, let's attach something to it. In the case of a fidget spinner, that would be some arms to spin it with. Listing 18.2 is a module for an arm.

```
module arm(){
    ArmWidth = 6;
    ArmLength = 12;
    HoleRadius = 6;
    translate([-ArmWidth / 2, WheelRadius - 1, 0]){
        difference(){
            union(){
                cube([ArmWidth, ArmLength, Height]);
                translate([ArmWidth / 2, ArmLength, 0])
                cylinder(h = Height, r = HoleRadius + 3);
```

```
      } // End of union
      translate ([ArmWidth / 2, ArmLength, - 1])
      cylinder(h = Height + 2,r = HoleRadius); //hole
    } // End of difference
  } // End of translate
} // End of arm module
```
Listing 18.2

This lets you set the width of the arm (the cube connecting the wheel to the outer ring) and the length of this arm, as well as the hole in the ring at the end of the arm, using defined constants. The width of the ring around the hole is set at 3 mm. The arm is translated away from the origin by the Radius of the wheel minus 1. This positions the arm on the outer edge of the wheel.

Since there are three arms, the modules are rotated around the wheel. The entire listing for the fidget spinner is shown in Listing 18.3. Figure 18.3 shows what it looks like.

```
AxleRadius = 11.25;
Height = 5;
WheelRadius = 15;
Gap = 1.25;
$fn = 99;

module Wheel(){

  cylinder(h = Height / 2, r1 = AxleRadius,
  r2 = AxleRadius + Height / 2);// Bottom of shaft

  translate([0, 0, Height / 2])
  cylinder(h = Height / 2, r1 = AxleRadius + Height / 2,
  r2 = AxleRadius); // Top of shaft
  difference(){
    cylinder(h = Height, r = WheelRadius); // Wheel
    cylinder(h = Height/2 + .001, r1 = AxleRadius + Gap,
    r2 = AxleRadius + Height / 2 + Gap); // Bottom of
    cutout
```

181

```
      translate([0, 0, Height / 2])
      cylinder(h = Height / 2, r1 = AxleRadius + Height / 2
      + Gap, r2 = AxleRadius + Gap); // Top of cutout

      translate([0, 0, -1])
      cylinder(h = Height + 2, r = AxleRadius + Gap);
      // Extend cutout
    } // End difference
} // End Wheel module

module arm(){
   ArmWidth = 6;
   ArmLength = 12;
   HoleRadius = 6;
   translate([-ArmWidth / 2, WheelRadius - 1, 0]){
      difference(){
         union(){
            cube([ArmWidth, ArmLength, Height]);
            translate([ArmWidth / 2, ArmLength, 0])
            cylinder(h = Height, r = HoleRadius + 3);
         } // End of union
         translate ([ArmWidth / 2, ArmLength, -1])
         cylinder(h = Height + 2, r = HoleRadius); //hole
      } // End of difference
   } // End of translate
} // End of arm module

Wheel();
arm();
rotate([0,0,120]) arm();
rotate([0,0,-120]) arm();
```
Listing 18.3

Figure 18.3

Chapter 19

Screw Threads

In this chapter I will discuss creating screw threads around a cylinder and also inside a hole to match the threads on the cylinder. This can allow you to make nuts and blots, but it also will allow you to make all sorts of parts that screw together. For example, you could create a rod with screw threads on each end and use it to connect two parts, or you could simply put a small cylinder with screw threads on one part and a hole with screw threads inside in on another part and screw them together.

First, let's look at just the bare screw threads themselves. This is shown in Figure 19.1.

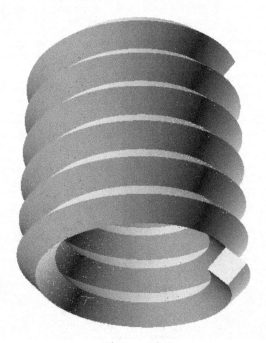

Figure 19.1

Notice that the threads are hollow. This is just the threads themselves, not the supporting cylinder. Listing 19.1 shows the module that creates just these screw threads.

```
ThreadHeight =  2;
Radius = 5;
Gap = .3;
degrees = 1;
CubeWidth = degrees * 2 * (Radius + ThreadHeight /
sqrt(2)) * PI / 360;

module Threads(TotalThreadHeight){

    for(a = [0 : degrees : 360 * (TotalThreadHeight /
    ThreadHeight + ThreadHeight)]){

    rotate([0, 0, a]) // Rotate around circle
    translate([0, 0, ThreadHeight * a / 360]) // Move up as
    you rotate
    rotate([atan(ThreadHeight / (2 * PI * (Radius +
    ThreadHeight / sqrt(2)))),0 , 0]) // Tilt cube slightly
    translate([Radius - ThreadHeight / 2, -CubeWidth / 2, 0])
    rotate([0, 45 , 0])
    cube([ThreadHeight / sqrt(2), CubeWidth, ThreadHeight
    / sqrt(2)]);

    } // End for
} //  End Threads module
```
                   Listing 19.1

The constant ThreadHeight sets the height of one thread. This would be the distance from one grove to another or one maximum extrusion to another. Radius is the radius of the screw. It is the radius from the middle of the screw to the inside (deepest part) of the grove, not to the maximum extension of the thread. If you want Radius to be the distance from the center to the maximum extension of the thread, change that line to read

185

Radius=5-ThreadHeight/2;

However, this will require you to make a few other changes in the code, which I will explain later. Generally, it is easiest to leave it the way I have written it.

Gap is the distance between the outside of the screw thread and the inside of the thread inside a hole, such as the hole in a bolt. The larger the gap, the easier it is to screw the threads into the hole, but the less tight the fit will be. Unlike previous models, you are not printing the pieces together, so you do not have to worry about the nut and bolt fusing together. This means that Gap can be much smaller. I find .3 to be a nice fit, but it can depend on how precise your printer is, so feel free to experiment. I will explain the constants degrees and CubeWidth (which is calculated and you should not tamper with) as I explain the code.

The module Threads has an input parameter TotalThreadHeight. This is the total height of the threads on the bolt or whatever you are attaching screw threads to. Note that this does not include the head of the bolt or screw or other part. I included this as a parameter so you can have varying lengths of screw parts in your project. I assume that other parameters, like radius, will be the same for all parts so that everything will fit together.

The only actual component of the Threads is a cube. However, this cube is recreated thousands of times using the for loop, and is modified from the last one. The cube itself is created by the code

cube([ThreadHeight/sqrt(2),CubeWidth,
ThreadHeight/sqrt(2)]).

CubeWidth, which was calculated at the beginning as a defined constant, is the width of the cube in the Y direction. Additional cubes will be added next to each cube, and this is calculated to be the ideal width for the cubes to fit together. The cube as created but this is shown in Figure 9.2.

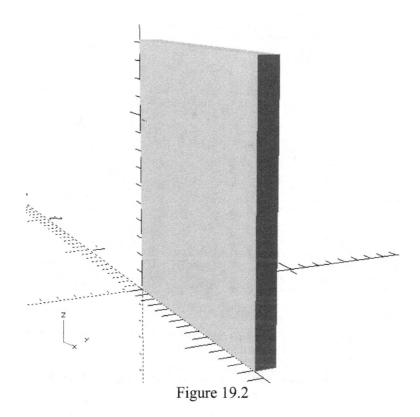

Figure 19.2

Next, the cube is rotated 45 degrees so that it becomes pointed in the horizontal direction. Remember that when long string of transitions is applied to a shape, the last ones (closest to the shape) are applied first. The result of this is shown in Figure 19.3.

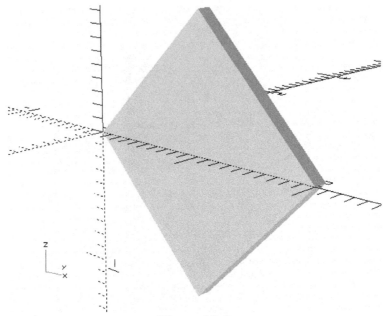

Figure 19.3

Next, the cube is translated. It is moved in the X direction by a distance of Radius - ThreadHeight/2. This puts the top and bottom of the rotated cube a distance of Radius from the center. This will be the groves of the screw. It is also moved CubeWidth / 2 in the negative Y direction, which centers it on the X axis. It is not moved in the Z direction at this time. The result is shown in Figure 19.4.

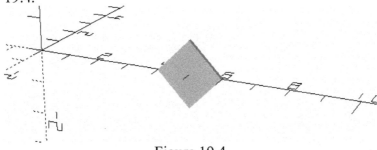

Figure 19.4

Next the cube is rotated by atan(ThreadHeight/(2 * PI * (Radius + ThreadHeight / sqrt(2)))) around the X axis.

This complicated equation tilts the edge of the cube a tiny amount so the edge is going in the direction of the screw threads. I will not bother to show a picture of this, since it is barely visible, but it does make the screw threads a tine bit smoother.

Now comes the fun part. Using the for operator with the variable a, the cube is duplicated over and over. Each new cube is raised by amount ThreadHeight*a/360 above the previous one by a translate command and moved around the Z axis by angle a. This creates the rotating slope you saw in Figure 19.1.

Now let's examine the for operator. It uses the variable named a. Any variable name of any number of letters could be used, but I chose a for angle. The amount it increases is degrees, the constant declared in the beginning of the code. I chose 1 degree as an appropriate amount. A larger number would result in less smooth thread, but faster rendering time. It keeps rotating until it reaches 360 * (TotalThreadHeight / ThreadHeight + ThreadHeight)]). This gives a thread slightly longer than the value you select for TotalThreadHeight, the height you want for your screw threads. The reason it is slightly longer is that, as you can see in Figure 19.1, the bottom (and top) end in a jagged point, and you will want to cut off a little of this to smooth out the top. You therefore need a little extra thread so you can trim it for the proper shape. I am about to get into this as I describe the CompleteThreads module which actually creates a cylinder of height TotalHeight with flat ends that you can attach to things, like a bolt head.

The CompleteThreads module is pretty simple. It generates the object shown in Figure 19.5 and is given in Listing 19.2.

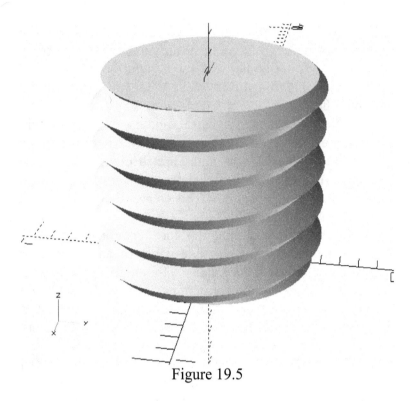
Figure 19.5

```
module CompleteThreads(TotalHeight){
  difference(){
    translate([0, 0, -ThreadHeight])
    Threads(TotalHeight);
    translate([0, 0, -ThreadHeight * 2])
    cylinder(h = ThreadHeight * 2, r = Radius +
    ThreadHeight);
    translate([0,0,TotalHeight])
    cylinder(h = ThreadHeight * 2, r = Radius +
    ThreadHeight);
  } // End difference
  cylinder(h=TotalHeight,r=Radius);
} // End CompleteThreads module
```
                    Listing 19.2

   This has an input parameter TotalHeight, which is
the height of the cylinder. It uses the difference command
to flatten out the top and bottom of the threads and add a

190

cylinder in the middle to make it solid. It takes the Threads module and gives it a value of the TotalHeight for the input parameter. It translates this downward a distance of ThreadHeight, and then chops off the top and bottom by providing the difference command with cylinders at the top and just below the X-Y plane at the bottom. It then puts a cylinder of height TotalHeight and radius Radius in the center.

Once you have this, you can mount it on anything. Listing 19.3 shows a module that creates a nut. It takes two parameters: ThreadsHeight, which is the height of the threads, and BaseHeight, which is the height of the six-sided base that is not part of the threads. The module simply creases the threaded cylinder using CompleteThreads, translates it up to the top of the base, and then creates the base using a six-sided cylinder. The result is the bolt shown in Figure 19.6.

```
module HexBolt(ThreadsHeight, BaseHeight){
    translate([0, 0, BaseHeight])
    CompleteThreads(ThreadsHeight);
    cylinder(h = BaseHeight, r = 2 * Radius, $fn = 6);
}
```

Listing 19.3

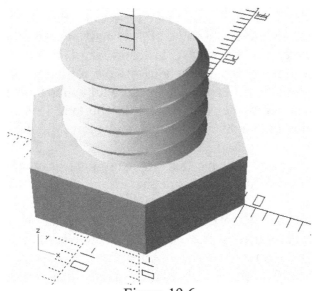

Figure 19.6

Now comes the slightly more complicated part about putting threads inside holes to put the bolt or other object into. First, we have the module ThreadsInside. This takes a parameter HoleHeight, which is how deep the hole is. The code is shown in Listing 19.4.

```
module ThreadsInside(HoleHeight){

  for(a = [0 : degrees : 360 * ((HoleHeight / ThreadHeight)
  + ThreadHeight)]){

    rotate([0, 0, a])
    translate([0, 0, ThreadHeight * a / 360])
    rotate([atan(ThreadHeight / (2 * PI * (Radius +
    ThreadHeight / sqrt(2)))), 0, 0])
    translate([Radius + Gap, -CubeWidth / 2, 0])
    rotate([0, 45, 0])
    cube([ThreadHeight / sqrt(2), CubeWidth,
    ThreadHeight / sqrt(2)]);

  } // End for
} // End ThreadsInside module
```

Listing 19.4

This is actually the same listing as the listing for Threads, with one exception. The radius of the threads has been increased from Radius − ThreadHeight / 2 in the outside threads to Radius + Gap. If Gap is 0, the inside threads would fit precisely in the outside threads. While this might be nice in theory if you had frictionless threads that precisely form in the exact shape of the model, in reality you need some space between the outer threads of the screw and the inner threads of the object it is screwed into. I find 0.3 comfortable.

Now we can fit the outside threads into something. You need use the difference command to create a hole in your object by removing a cylinder of radius Radius + ThreadHeight / 2 from the object you are putting the threads into. Then you insert the threads of the height as the hole into the hole. Listing 19.5 demonstrates this with a hex nut.

```
module Nut(NutHeight){
   difference(){ // Outer body of nut
      cylinder(h = NutHeight, r = Radius * 2, $fn = 6);
      translate([0, 0, -1])
      cylinder(h = NutHeight + 2, r = Radius +
      ThreadHeight / 2, $fn=99);
   } // End difference
   translate([0, 0, -ThreadHeight])
   difference(){ //Threads
      ThreadsInside(NutHeight);
      translate([0, 0, NutHeight + ThreadHeight])
      cylinder(h = NutHeight, r = Radius * 2, $fn = 6);
      translate([0, 0, -NutHeight + ThreadHeight])
      cylinder(h = NutHeight, r = Radius * 2, $fn = 6);
   } // End difference
} // End Nut module
```

Listing 19.5

The first difference command simply creates a hexagonal shape with a cylinder cut out of the middle. The second difference takes the ThreadsInside module and cuts off the top and bottom just like we did to create CompleteThreads, except that we do not insert a cylinder into the threads to fill the area inside the threads for this, since we want hollow threads. You can do exactly the same thing with any shape. You simply use that shape in place of cylinder(h = NutHeight, r = Radius * 2, $fn = 6); as the body. Incidentally, it is not necessary for the hole to go all the way through if you want to simply screw something into something.

Chapter 20

Snap In

In the previous chapter, I talked about making parts you could connect by screwing them together. In this chapter, I will show how to make parts that snap together. The basic snap is shown in Figure 20.1.

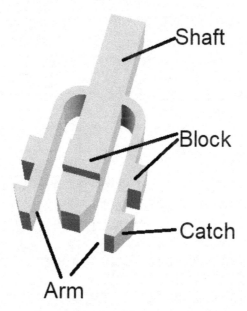

Figure 20.1

The snap is inserted into a rectangular hole, the arms bend inward to allow the catches to slide into the hole, then the arms bend back out and the catches prevent the snap from sliding back out. The blocks prevent it from sliding any farther in. You attach whatever you want to the shaft. Notice the curve where the arms meet the shaft. This curve makes the arms bend inward more easily than a right angle. The code for this entire snap is shown in Listing 20.1.

```
// Next 3 constants are characteristics of hole
PlugThickness = 3; // Thickness of the surface you are
plugging into
PlugHoleLength = 16; // Length of hole
PlugHoleWidth = 8; // Width of hole
// Next 3 are Gap margins
PlugHoleLengthGap = .3;
PlugHoleWidthGap = .4;
PlugThicknessGap = .6; // Gap along thickness of surface

ArmLength = PlugThickness + 14; // Length of bending
arm
ArmWidth = 1.5; // Width of bending arm
Height = PlugHoleWidth - PlugHoleWidthGap;
ShaftWidth = PlugHoleLength - 9;
ShaftLength = 30;

module SnapArm(){

  translate([PlugHoleLength / 2 – ArmWidth -
  PlugHoleLengthGap, 0, 0])
  cube([ArmWidth, ArmLength, Height]); // Main arm

  // The following difference code is the loop
  difference(){
    intersection(){
      translate([ShaftWidth / 2, ArmLength, 0])
      cylinder(h = Height, r = PlugHoleLength / 2 -
      PlugHoleLengthGap – ShaftWidth / 2, $fn = 99);

      translate([ShaftWidth / 2, ArmLength, 0])
      cube([PlugHoleLength / 2, PlugHoleLength / 2,
      Height]);
    } // End intersection
```

```
    translate([ShaftWidth / 2, ArmLength, -1])
    cylinder(h = Height + 2, r = PlugHoleLength / 2 -
    PlugHoleLengthGap – ShaftWidth / 2 –
    ArmWidth, $fn = 99);
    } // End loop difference

    translate([PlugHoleLength / 2 - PlugHoleLengthGap,
    PlugThickness + PlugThicknessGap + 3.75, 0])
    cube([2, 4, Height]); // Side plug

    // The following difference is the catch
    translate([PlugHoleLength / 2 - PlugHoleLengthGap, 0,
    0])
    difference(){

        cube([2, 3.75, Height]);

        translate([0, 0, -1.5]) rotate([0, 0, -30])
        cube([3 * sqrt(2), 6, 13.5]);
    } // End difference
} // End module SnapArm

module FullSnap(){

    // The following cube and cylinder are the shaft
    translate([-ShaftWidth / 2, 4, 0])
    cube([ShaftWidth, ShaftLength, Height]);

    translate([0, 4, 0])
    cylinder(h = Height, d = ShaftWidth, $fn = 6);

    // The following two lines are the arms
    SnapArm();
    mirror([1, 0, 0])SnapArm();

    translate([-ShaftWidth / 2, PlugThickness +
    PlugThicknessGap + 3.75, Height])
```

```
    cube([ShaftWidth, 4, 2 + PlugHoleWidthGap]); // Center
block
} // End module FullSnap

FullSnap();
```

Listing 20.1

First you have the defined constants. PlugThickness is the thickness of the surface you have a hole in to plug the snap into. This is the variable you are most likely to want to change. Then you have PlugHoleLength and PlugHoleWidth, the length and width of the hole. You might want to change these, but be aware that changing these too much can distort the entire plug. Then you have the gap constants, the ones that control how much extra room you are leaving around the snap. PlugThicknessGap is the gap added to the distance between the catches and the side and front blocks.

I have made ArmLength automatically adjust to the PlugThickness because as PlugThickness increases, the blocks move up the arms and I want to make sure the arms are long enough that the blocks do not move off the arms. However, you can adjust the arm length by changing the number that is currently 14. The longer the arms are, the less you have to bend them to allow the snap to go into the hole. ArmWidth is the thickness of the arms. The thicker they are, the stronger they are but the harder it is to bend them. I find that 1.5 is tough enough to hold the snap in place but thin enough to bend easily. Of course, how easily they bend will depend on other factors, like the material you use, the infill, etc. Height is the height of the shaft and arms as it lays on the print bed, which means it is the thickness when it is standing up. ShaftWidth and ShaftLength are the width and length of the center shaft. Changing the length does not affect the print as long as it is long enough for the arms to connect to. The width does because making it wider without changing anything else decreases the distance between the shaft and the arms, making them harder to bend. I therefore linked it to the PlugHoleLength, which controls the spacing of the arms. You can fiddle with that if you like, but remember that the shaft you use for the snap does not have to be the entire shaft or other object you are connecting it to. You can use a short shaft and put whatever you want, like a thicker or thinner shaft, at the end of it.

The main code has two modules. The first creates the arms. Since there are two arms, making one arm a module and then mirroring it to make the second arm greatly simplifies the coding. The second module is the one that connects the arms and all the other pieces to form the entire snap.

To make the arm, first I added the cube that is the main body of the arm. Then I added the loop at the top. The loop is formed by first intersecting a short cylinder with a cube t hat intersects in the upper right quarter of the cylinder, forming a quarter of a disk. Then I use difference to cut out the center with a cylinder of smaller radius and the center at the same point as the larger cylinder. This forms a fourth of a circle, which is the arc.

The side block is just a cube stuck on the side. The catch is formed by taking cube and then using difference to cut away a corner, creating a wedge shape. That completes the arm module. All of these components are built the appropriate distance from the center, so you do not have to move them when you attached the arm to the shaft.

For the FullSnap module, I first add the large cube that is the main body if the shaft. I add a six-sided cylinder to this to extend it down a bit farther. Why not just have the large cube go down farther? The corners could block the arms when you bend them, restricting how far you can bend them to clear the sides of the hole. The shaft will still block the arms eventually, but having the bottom corners slope inward like this gives you a little extra room.

Next, I add the first arm, then a mirror of this to make the second arm. Finally, I add a cube to the shaft to form the center block. Figure 20.2 shows the snap inserted into a test surface, a simple flat cube with a hole in it.

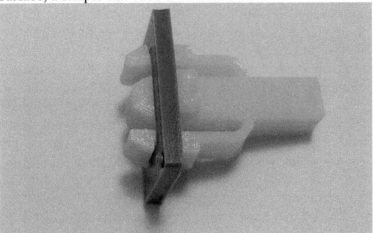

Figure 20.2

Chapter 21

Gears

In this chapter, I will discuss making gears. This will be a simple example of using the for operator. It is actually a simplified version of making the screw threads. You simply create a pointed shape a distance from the origin, and then rotate it around a circle to make the teeth. Then you fill in the rest of the gear. The simple code is shown in Listing 21.1

```
Radius = 15;
GearHeight = 4;
Teeth = 30;
ToothSize = (1.15 * Radius * PI) / (Teeth);

module Gear(Size){

  // The following for operation makes the teeth
  for(a = [0 : 360/(Teeth * Size) : 360 - 360/(Teeth * Size)])

  rotate([0, 0, a])
  translate([Radius * Size + ToothSize * .43, 0, 0])
  cylinder(h = GearHeight, r = ToothSize, $fn = 3);

  // The following cylinder fills in center of gear
  cylinder(h = GearHeight, r = Radius * Size, $fn = 99);

  // This cylinder is the shaft. You will almost certainly
  change this
  cylinder(h = GearHeight + 5, r = 2, $fn = 99);

} // End Gear
```

```
Gear(1);
```

There are three defined constants that you can easily change. Radius is the radius of the gear. It is specifically the radius of the inner point of the teeth, not the outer edge of the teeth. That is, Radius is the distance from the center of the gear to the inner grove of the teeth. GearHeight is the height of the gear lying on its side, which is the thickness of the gear. Teeth is the number of teeth around the gear. The more teeth you have, the smaller each one is. The defined constant ToothSize is calculated automatically to get the specified number of teeth around a gear with the specified radius.

The code is put into a module called Gear to easily allow you to make several gears. This module takes the Size parameter. Size is expressed as a ratio. A Size value of 1 gives you a gear with the radius specified by Radius and the number of teeth specified by Teeth. A Size value of 2 would give you gear with twice that radius and twice as many teeth. A Size value of .5 would give you a gear with a radius of half the value of Radius and half as many teeth, and so on. This allows you to automatically create gears that mesh together. If you create a gear with Size 1 and another gear with Size .5 but all the other constants the same, the larger gear will fit with the smaller gear but the smaller gear will turn twice as fast because it has half as many gears. Thus, this module makes it easy to make gear trains. Note that if you plan to make smaller gears this way, it is a good idea to pick a value of Teeth that has lots of even divisors. For example, 30 can be divided by 2, 3, 5, 6, 10, 12, and 20. You would not use all these options, of course. For example, using a Size of .5 (dividing by 20), would give you a gear with 3 teeth, which would not work. It is probably best to start out by creating your smallest gear, and then using numbers greater than 1 for Size for the other gears.

Getting back to the code, the first part uses a for operator to creates a circle of triangular shapes. Each shape is created using the cylinder command cylinder(h = GearHeight, r = ToothSize, $fn = 3). Remember that $fn defines how many sides the cylinder has. Normally you make this very large to create a very round cylinder, but you can use a small number, like 3, to create a specific shape. One triangle created by this is shown in Figure 21.1.

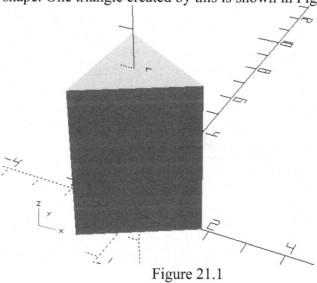

Figure 21.1

The translate([Radius * Size + ToothSize * .43, 0, 0]) moves the triangle out to a distance of Radius from the center. Radius is multiplied by Size so that the distance is increased or decreased if Size is not 1, thus increasing or decreasing the radius of the gear. The amount ToothSize*.43 is added because it is the center of the triangle that is moved by the distance Radius * Size, and the added distance moves the triangle so that it is the closest point that is at the Radius distance.

The rotate([0, 0, a]) command rotates the triangle around the circumference of the gear as angle a increases. The for operator increases the angle a. It starts at angle 0. It increases by 360 degrees divided by Teeth * Size. This means that the larger the number of teeth, the smaller the amount the angle increases. This makes sense, since the more teeth on the gear, the closer together they must be. Remember that the number of teeth increases as Size increases, which is why Teeth is multiplied by Size. The final tooth is put at 360 –360 / (Teeth * Size). This means that the final tooth is put at the end of the circle around the gear minus the size of that last tooth. Note that there is no opening and closing squiggly brackets for this for statement, because it applies to only one shape, and therefore there is no need to enclose the objects the for operator is applied to. The result of this for operator acting on the rotate command controlling the triangle is shown in Figure 21.1.

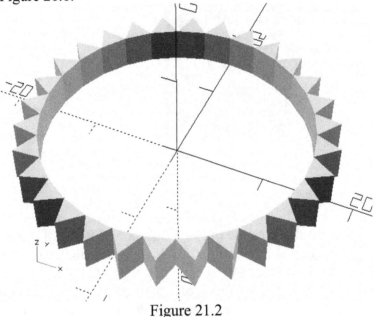

Figure 21.2

You now have the teeth of the gear. The line
cylinder(h = GearHeight, r = Radius * Size, $fn = 99);
creates a cylinder that fills in the inside of the gear. The line
cylinder(h = GearHeight + 5, r = 2, $fn = 99);
creates a shaft. The addition of these two parts is shown in Figure 21.3.

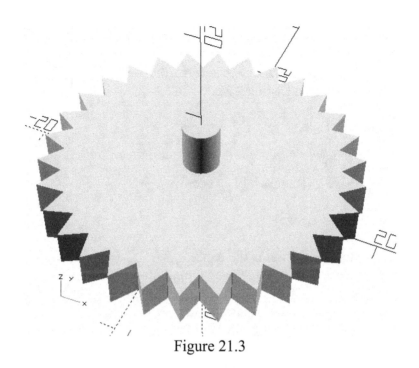

Figure 21.3

You will almost certainly want to change the shaft line to change the radius and length of the shaft for your application. You can also change the shaft into a hole that you can put a separate shaft through by changing

```
cylinder(h = GearHeight, r =  Radius * Size, $fn = 99);
cylinder(h = GearHeight + 5, r = 2, $fn = 99);
```

into

```
difference(){
    cylinder(h = GearHeight, r = Radius * Size, $fn = 99);

    translate([0, 0, -1])
    cylinder(h = GearHeight + 2, r = 2, $fn = 99);
    }
```

205

In Listing 21.1, I used a triangle to form the teeth. Instead of using a triangle, you could use a square by using $fn=4 for the cylinders that form the teeth. The code for this is shown in Listing 21.2.

```
Radius = 15;
GearHeight = 4;
Teeth = 30;
ToothSize = (Radius * PI) / Teeth;

module Gear(Size){

    // This for section is the teeth
    for(a = [0 : 360 / (Teeth * Size) : 360 – 360 / (Teeth *
    Size)])
    rotate([0, 0, a]) translate([Radius * Size, 0, 0])
    cylinder(h = GearHeight, r = ToothSize, $fn = 4);

    cylinder(h = GearHeight, r = Radius * Size + ToothSize /
    (Teeth * .65), $fn = 99); // Fill in center of gear

  //This cylinder is the shaft. You will almost certainly
change this
    cylinder(h = GearHeight + 5, r = 2, $fn = 99);

} // End Gear

Gear(1);
```

Listing 21.2

This is very much like the first gear in Listing 21.1. It is not necessary to tweak the ToothSize or the X parameter in the translate command before the cylinder that forms the tooth. This is because the center of the square is located right where you want the radius of the gear to be. The result of the right of teeth formed by the for operator is shown in Figure 21.4. Of course, I am leaving out the cylinder that fills in the gear in this figure to allow you to see the teeth more clearly.

Figure 21.4

Notice the difference between this and Figure 21.2. The main effect of using the square instead of the triangle is that the teeth are more pointed. That is, they extend out farther with the triangle. Actually, you can control exactly how far the teeth extend out using Listing 21.2 by adding scale([n,1,1]), where n is any number, just before the cylinder that forms the teeth. For example, making the for line read

rotate([0, 0, a]) translate([Radius * Size, 0, 0])
scale([2, 1, 1])
cylinder(h = GearHeight, r = ToothSize, $fn = 4);

gives you the shape shown in Figure 21.5.

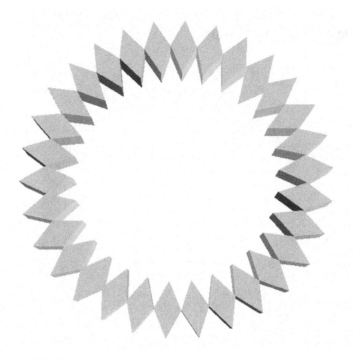

Figure 21.5

You can see that the teeth have become elongated and much shaper. By adjusting the number that you scale the X parameter by, you can make the teeth exactly like you want them.

You can also adjust the teeth to be actual square teeth rather than points by rotating the tooth cylinder 45 degrees and increasing the spacing between teeth in the for operator as shown in Listing 21.3. This gives you the figure shown in Figure 21.6.

```
Radius = 15;
GearHeight = 4;
Teeth = 30;
ToothSize = (Radius * PI) / Teeth;

module Gear(Size){
```

```
for(a = [0 : 360 / (Teeth * Size) * 1.5 : 360-360 / (Teeth
* Size)])
rotate([0, 0, a]) translate([Radius * Size, 0, 0])
scale([2, 1,1])
rotate([0, 0, 45])
cylinder(h = GearHeight, r = ToothSize, $fn = 4);

cylinder(h = GearHeight, r = Radius * Size + ToothSize /
(Teeth * .65), $fn = 99);  // Fill in center of gear

// This cylinder is the shaft. You will almost certainly
change this
cylinder(h = GearHeight + 4, r = 2, $fn = 99);

} // End Gear

Gear(1);
```

Listing 21.3

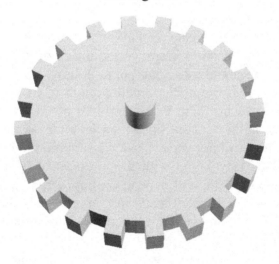

Figure 21.6

There are all sorts of way you can have fun with
this gear code. Feel free to experiment.

Chapter 22

Hollow objects

There are several reasons why you might want to create completely sealed hollow objects. You might want to make the object very light, for example, if you want it to float well. On the other hand, you might want to make it heavy by filling it with something like sand. You can do this by creating a hollow object, pausing the print just before the printer gets to the top, filling the object, and then resuming the print. You can also fill it with a substance like plaster of Paris to make it stronger. You can also insert things into it to make it rattle. Finally, you might want to make a watertight sealed container to put something like an electronic device in.

You can create a hollow object by using the difference command to remove the inside of the model. If all you care about is having some hollow space, this can just be a cube or cylinder small enough to fit inside your object. However, there is the problem of the unsupported top of the hollow space. Since the whole idea is f or it to be hollow, you will not want to use the support option on your slicer. This leaves you with the question of whether you need support. This will depend on how large an area you are hollowing out, what material you are using, the quality of your printer, and your slicer settings. I have run tests that show that some of my printers can bridge a gap of at least 35 mm across an open space. If the maximum distance across your open space is short enough, you may be able to get away with simply using difference to carve out an empty space.

If the distance is too long, you can have the top of the empty space slope, rather than being flat. As described before, 3D printers can print areas without anything directly under them provided they slope gradually into the overhang instead of going horizontally.

Suppose you want to cut out a cylindrical area. In that case, cutting out a cone pointed upward on top of the cylinder will eliminate the problem by providing a gentle slope rather than going straight across.

For purposes of demonstration, lets assume you want a hollow cylinder. Figure 22.1 shows a cutout cross-section of this. The code in Listing 22.1 will provide that.

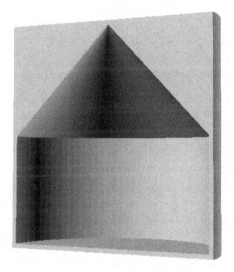

Figure 22.1

```
$fn = 99;
OuterRadius = 50;
OuterHeight = 100;
WallThickness = 2;
InnerRadius = OuterRadius - WallThickness;
A = 45;
ConeHeight = InnerRadius * cos(A) / sin(A);
InnerHeight = (OuterHeight – 2 * WallThickness) -
ConeHeight;
module HollowCylinder(){
    difference(){
        cylinder(h = OuterHeight, r = OuterRadius);
```

```
        translate([0, 0, WallThickness])
        cylinder(h = InnerHeight, r = InnerRadius);

        translate([0, 0, WallThickness + InnerHeight - .001])
        cylinder(h = ConeHeight, r1 = InnerRadius, r2 = 0);
    } // End difference
} // End HollowCylinder module

HollowCylinder();
```

Listing 22.1

Here, $fn is, as explained previously, the number of sides of the cylinder. We want a smooth cylinder, so we are using a large number of sides. OuterRadius is the radius of your actual cylinder, and OuterHeight is the height. WallThickness is the thickness of the walls you want for your cylinder, the distance from the outside of the cylinder to the hollow area. InnerRadius is the radius of the hollowed out area, and is calculated by simply subtracting the desired wall thickness from the outer radius. This assumes that the outer shape is a cylinder. If it is not, you can manually define the inner radius as any size that will fit within your outer object with a bit of room around it to provide walls.

The constant A is the angle that you feel your printer can print a slope at without it caving in. An angle of 90 would be printing straight across horizontally, bridging the distance directly. You could use this if you think your printer can bridge the diameter of the cylinder without a slope. An angle of 0 would be a wall going straight up. An angle A of 45 would mean the print is going horizontally at the same rate it is rising vertically. You can determine what angle works for your printer, material, etc. experimentally, or just pick a fairly safe number like 45. ConeHeight is the height of the cone, and is calculated from the radius inner cutout cylinder and the angle you have chosen for the slope. InnerHeight is the height of the inner cylinder cutout. Note that the shorter the cone, the taller the cylinder can be.

The code is then very simple. You create the outer shape, in this case a cone but it could be any shape that a cone cutout would fit into well. You use difference to remove the main cylinder. The dimensions of this cylinder are InnerHeight and InnerRadius, as previously defined. Note that it is translated up by WallThickness so that the bottom has this thickness too. You then also remove the cone, which has the previously calculated height of ConeHeight. The radius of the bottom of the cone is the same as the radius of the main cylinder cutout. The radius of the top is 0. That is all there is to it.

Suppose the object you are creating is more rectangular shaped, so you want more of a cube-shaped hollow area to be hollowed out. Again, you want a sloping top area to avoid needing supports. Figure 22.2 shows a rectangular shape hollowed out in this way.

Figure 22.2

The code for this is very similar to the code for the cylinder-shaped hollow area, at least in principle. It is shown in Listing 22.2.

OuterX = 20;

```
OuterY = 30;
OuterHeight = 50;
WallThickness = 2;
InnerX = OuterX – 2 * WallThickness;
InnerY = OuterY – 2 * WallThickness;
A = 45;
TopHeight = InnerX * (cos(A) / sin(A));
BottomHeight = OuterHeight – 2 * WallThickness –
TopHeight / 2;

module HollowCube(){

  difference(){

    // The following cube line is whatever object you are
    hollowing out. You will probably replace it with a
    union of other shapes
    cube([OuterX, OuterY, OuterHeight]);

    translate([WallThickness, WallThickness,
    WallThickness])
    cube([InnerX, InnerY, BottomHeight]);

    translate([WallThickness, WallThickness,
    WallThickness + BottomHeight - .001])
    resize([InnerX, InnerY, TopHeight])
    rotate([0, 45, 0]) cube(1);

  } // End difference
} // End HollowCube module

HollowCube();
```
Listing 22.2

The constants OuterX, OuterY, and OuterHeight are simply the outer dimensions of the object you are trying to hollow out in the X, Y, and Z direction. If the object is irregular in shape (not a simple rectangular object), these

214

should all be the minimum of any part of the object in that direction. WallThickness is the minimum thickness you want between the hollow area and the outside of the object. InnerX and InnerY are the dimensions of the hollowed-out area. In this example, these are calculated from the outer dimensions. However, if your object is very irregular, you can skip inputting OuterX, OuterY, OuterHeight and WallThickness and just provide InnerX and InnerY yourself by deciding how much area you want to hollow out.

As with the hollowed-out cylinder, A is the angle you feel comfortable sloping the top of you hollowed out area without support material. TopHeight is the height of the sloping area at the top. As you can see from the equation InnerX * (cos(A) / sin(A)), it is calculated from the angle A and, in the example, InnerX. I say that you use InnerX in this example because you must use the shorter of InnerX and InnerY. Note that in this example, the X dimension of your outer object, and therefore the inner hollowed out area, is smaller, so you use that. If you use the longer dimension, the angle of the slope at the top will not be correct, and in some extreme cases there will be a hole at the bottom of your model. So, if InnerY is shorter than InnerX, change the equation to
TopHeight = InnerY * (cos(A) / sin(A));
The next line calculates the height of the rectangular area under the sloping area. If you want to set your own height rather than having it calculated from the outer height of your model, change the line to read
BottomHeight = InnerHeight − TopHeight / 2;
where you replace InnerHeight with a number that is the total height you want the hollowed-out area to be, such as
BottomHeight = 40 − TopHeight / 2;
Note that the number for the inner height should be the total height of the area you want hollowed out, including the slanted area at the top.

The module that creates your hollowed out object then takes the object you are hollowing out and uses the difference command to subtract the top and bottom part of the hollowing out shape. When writing this, you must be sure that the object you are hollowing out is a single object. That is, you must combine all the parts into one object, either a union or a module. If you simply list the parts in the first part of the difference group, some of the parts of your model will be subtracted rather than added. This applies to the cylindrical hollowed out model too.

In these examples, I have created the models as modules and then added the module to have it displayed. This is not really necessary. You could leave out enclosing the whole thing in a module and just used the difference command.

Chapter 23

Lovers

So far, I have concentrated on giving examples of projects that are practical as well as educational. Just for fun, I would like to wrap up with an art project. It is a little piece I call Lovers. Using the linear_extrude command with the twist feature, it creates two columns twisting and winding around each other like intertwined lovers. Figure 23.1 shows two variations on this.

Figure 23.1

The code for the one on the left is shown in Listing 23.1.

```
translate([-15, -10, 0]) cube([15, 20, 5]); // Base 1

translate([0, 0, 5])
linear_extrude(height = 50, twist = 360, slices = 200)
translate([-5, 0, 0]) square(9.5, center = true); //Swirl 1

translate([0, -10, 0]) cube([15, 20, 5]); //base 2
```

```
translate([0, 0, 5])
linear_extrude(height = 50, twist = 360, slices = 200)
translate([5, 0, 0]) square(9.5, center = true); //Swirl 2
```
Listing 23.1

First, we have the base, the simple cube at the bottom. Then we have the swirl. Remember that the commands are executed in reverse order, starting with the end and working back to the beginning. So, first we have square(9.5, center = true) which gives a 2D square, 9.5 mm by 9.5 mm. Remember that when you only list one length parameter instead of a list surrounded by square brackets, that one length applies to all directions. Because I included center = true, the square is centered on the origin. Next the translate([-5, 0, 0]) command moves this −5 mm in the X direction. Then the linear_extrude(height = 50, twist = 360, slices = 200) performs the extruding operation. It extrudes up a distance of 50 mm, goes around the X-Y axis by 360 degrees, and has 200 slices to give it some pretty good resolution. The scale parameter is not given, so a value of 1 is the default, which means that the top is the same size as the bottom. Finally, the spiral is translated up 5 mm by the translate command, which sets the spiral on top of the base, which is 5 mm high. This creates one of the spirals. For clarity, Figure 23.2 shows this one part of the figure.

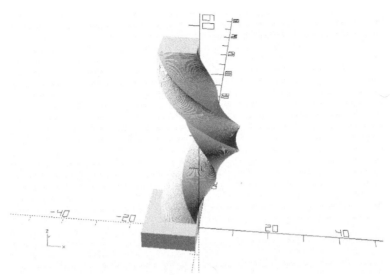

Figure 23.2

The next half of the code simply duplicates the first half, only displacing it slightly. Notice that the base cube is not moved –15 mm on the X-axis, but left in its original position on that axis, although it is still moved –10 mm on the Y-axis to center it on that axis. The cube that forms the base of the spiral is 5 mm on the X-axis instead of –5 mm. This positions the spirals so that they intertwine.

The three-color art piece on the left side of Figure 23.1 was made by making each spiral separately and using a different color filament. Then the base was made simply by creating a rectangular shape with a rectangular hole in the center to fit the two spirals into. The code for the base is given in Listing 23.2.

```
difference(){
    cube([50, 40, 10]);
    translate([9.5, 9.5, 5])cube([31, 21, 10]);
}
```

Listing 23.2